Boston: the job ahead

*A publication of the Joint Center
for Urban Studies of the
Massachusetts Institute of Technology
and Harvard University*

D1447864

Boston:

the job ahead

Martin Meyerson and Edward C. Banfield

HARVARD UNIVERSITY PRESS · CAMBRIDGE, MASSACHUSETTS · 1966

Contents

Illustrations and Credits

Maps

Introduction: A Point of View

The American city — so we are told from every side — is in a state of crisis. Its residential neighborhoods are blighted, its streets congested, its economy moribund, its services deficient, and its government ineffective. The "urban crisis" will soon, it is said, produce an "urban catastrophe."

Anyone who, after reading about the ills of the city and its surrounding area, opened his eyes and looked about him, expecting to find misery everywhere, would be surprised. He would find much that is right with the metropolis. He would find that considerably more than half of the families in metropolitan areas live in houses which they own, something that urban people all over the world would like to do. More than three quarters have cars which they drive to work, to play, and to shop. In the American metropolis there are more white-collar workers than blue-collar ones, more children who will graduate from high school than will not (and more who will go on to universities and colleges than in the rest of the world), and more discretionary income than subsistence income in the average family budget. ("Discretionary" income is income not required to provide a minimum level of food, clothing, and shelter.) The amount of publicly provided services has practically doubled since the Second World War and is higher than in any other large country. If some public services are less than adequate, the reason is likely to be that a majority of the citizens has voted against them. For American cities and suburbs, unlike those of almost all other democratic countries, are in the main governed by their electorates and not by the national government.

Even if it is understood that what the critics have in mind is not the American metropolis in general but only certain cities — the larger central cities and the larger, older suburbs — indeed, even if they have in mind only the poorest parts of these areas, the situation is not as bad as it is sometimes made out to be. True, there is dilapidated urban housing, but the amount declined between 1950 and 1960. With notable exceptions, the high-density slum — the "teeming" slum, as it used to be called — is less dense. There are many poor people in the metropolis, but the percentage of them has declined, despite the steady inflow of low-income people from rural areas and small towns and the high birth rate among the poor. Private enterprise has not provided all widely desired services and facilities, but city planning and state and national programs have begun to fill the gaps.

Far from being a catastrophe, the American metropolis is a great achievement — one of the great achievements of all time — if judged from its success in giving scores of millions of people what they want. If what these millions choose — single-family houses and private cars, for example — results in costs such as traffic congestion, or increases in air pollution, these costs should not overshadow the achievements. For the potentialities of the American metropolis are only beginning to unfold, and it is within our power, in the next twenty years, to minimize the costs of urban development while we maximize the achievements. We believe that this can happen, despite a continued increase in urban population.

Boston is an example of a community which is far from facing impending disaster. As we shall demonstrate in the chapters which follow, metropolitan Boston is an attractive, comfortable, and convenient place. Its economy has again and again met and overcome new handicaps, and prospered. Its highway and transit systems are basically sound. It is not a haven for crime and delinquency. The organization of its governments is sounder than generally credited. Public programs such as urban renewal, after starting out with serious mistakes, have become humane. The region's architectural and landscape heritage makes it one of the most aesthetically satisfying metropolitan areas anywhere. Compared to situations in other American cities (not the standard that we would wish for, of course) the position of Negroes and other minority groups is improving.

This is not to say that all is right with the Boston area or other urban areas in America. Our purpose is to point out much that is wrong, and to suggest things we think should be done to improve matters.

Our reason for inveighing here against the crisis view of the metropolis is that if taken literally it leads to foolish and futile policy prescriptions. A balanced point of view, one which sees what is right with the metropolis as well as what is wrong with it, is essential if one is to make recommendations that are sensible and workable and likely to make matters better rather than worse. (Possibly the crisis view is advanced because its advocates believe the city would get attention only through hyperbole, since there are many competing causes. We reject such cynicism.)

A failing of the crisis view of the city is that it disposes one to try to do something in situations where nothing needs to be done. "Solving" pseudo problems would be a harmless enough, although expensive, waste of time if there were no danger of inadvertently creating a real problem, or of making a real problem worse. In our opinion, this danger is very genuine.

Another trouble with the crisis view is that it leads to *ad hoc* remedies and nostrums. If indeed catastrophe impends, then "crash programs" are called for. One cannot, of course, take time to examine alternative courses of action, or to consider what the unintended consequences of a program may be for various aspects of urban life other than the one on which attention is focused. Nor can one consider carefully whether the measures proposed are at all likely to attain even the limited ends sought. The crisis-monger and the nostrum-monger work together as partners.

The approach that we recommend, and that we have tried to exemplify in this book, is one which views the metropolis as a complicated system of interrelated elements. The state of one element in the system is largely and sometimes wholly determined by that of others. (One cannot, for example, significantly reduce air pollution without affecting the location of certain industries and transportation routes, and therefore without affect-

1. The center of Boston as seen by Malcolm Woronoff, Aerial Photos of New England, looking westward from a plane over Logan Airport, summer of 1965.

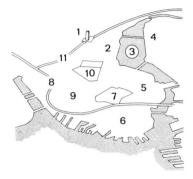

1. Prudential Center
2. Back Bay
3. Charles River
4. Cambridge
5. West End
6. North End
7. Government Center (under construction)
8. Central Artery
9. Financial district
10. Boston Common
11. Massachusetts Turnpike Extension

A Point of View

4

ing employment, tax revenues, and traffic.) Some elements of the system are relatively unchanging and predictable; others are in flux and unpredictable. Some are within the power of the local government (the elected officials or the electorate itself) to change; others have to be taken as fixed features of the situation, at least in the short run. In order to analyze the problems of cities and suburbs in a manner that might help guide policy, one must make many judgments both about the relative importance of the various elements of the system and about the possibility that they will change or can be changed by government. Some of these judgments can be made easily and with a high degree of certainty (for example, it is safe to say that for the next couple of decades there will be sizable Negro populations in most of the larger central cities). Others are highly problematic. (Will race prejudice decline or increase in the next twenty years?) Ideally, in a book of this kind, one ought to be very explicit about the factual assumptions on which the argument rests and ought to indicate what degree of confidence one attaches to each of them. We have not been able to do so. We have endeavored, however, to base our policy recommendations on a fairly complete and internally consistent account of things as they are and as, in our opinion, they ought to be. The reader will find that again and again we call for a general strategy to deal with the large systems of activities which make up the contemporary metropolis.

Judgments about what is politically possible, or what might become so in the next few years, are especially hazardous. It is fatuous to recommend banning private cars from the downtown districts if the people of the community would not stand for it. The temptation is to conclude that anything not taken seriously at present by leading politicians is politically out of the question. But of course politicians, including leading ones, make mistakes. Political reality, moreover, now and then changes with remarkable speed, sometimes in response to the "leadership" of people who insisted on trying to do what was (to begin with) politically impossible. Whatever the errors of judgment we may have made in these matters, they have not been those of the advocate who represents something as politically possible in the hope that by doing this he can make it so. Even where our own policy predilections are most involved, we have tried to be realistic. At the same time, we have kept in mind that a policy-proposing enterprise like this one rests on the assumption that some matters, including some important ones, are open to political change.

Another way of characterizing our general approach is to say that it is an economizing one. We mean by this that we start from the assumption that nothing is free — that getting something one wants always involves giving up something else that one wants — and then go on to look for the best terms that can be made. One who adopts this approach does not simply look for a way of achieving some given end, say the reduction of traffic congestion. Instead he looks for that way, among the many possible ways, which will achieve the end with the least possible sacrifice of other ends (e.g., the least inconvenience and expense to motorists, safety hazards, administrative cost, and so on). He is therefore always engaged in an effort to measure and compare the costs and benefits (nonmonetary as well as monetary, of course) of doing things one way with those of doing them other ways.

This preoccupation with finding the most economical (which is to say, most satisfying) way of doing things leads us to favor the widest possible use of the market and the price mechanism for publicly provided as well as privately provided goods and services. Where the problem of policy is to give the individual what he prefers (as distinguished from what someone thinks he ought to have) there is a great deal to be said for arranging the situation so that people can bid against each other for what they want. We are aware, of course, that inequities in the distribution of income limit the advantages of the market as a rationing device. With respect to many of the commodities under discussion here, however, the costs are small, so that even low-income families would not be seriously affected by using the market mechanism. For example, a rise in the price of a transit ride from 20 cents to 25 cents, although it is 25 percent, would not entail great hardship.

A more serious limitation on the use of the price mechanism is that it is impossible to apply it in many situations. (One cannot, for example, offer to sell each individual whatever amount of air-pollution reduction he would like to buy; the air of the city must be purified for everyone if it is purified for anyone.)

Another serious limitation on the use of the price mechanism is that there are a good many matters in which the problem of policy is to give the individual not what he wants but what the authorities think he should have. No one believes in trying to give the morally incompetent—viz., children, lunatics, criminals —whatever they want. Everyone recognizes, too, that there are situations in which morally competent people must be required to consume (and perhaps also to pay for) goods and services which they would not choose to buy if left to themselves. The justification for this is, of course, that neighbors or the community at large would be adversely affected otherwise. We are not in the least opposed to measures which constrain the individual in order to promote the common good. We do strongly believe, however, that the burden of proof is on those who assert that the advantages to the community or society are sufficient to justify infringing the freedom of the morally competent individual. We must ask ourselves what, precisely, are these advantages and to whom will they accrue? What, precisely, are to be the infringements of freedom and to whom will *they* accrue?

Although we shall be talking about the problems of metropolitan Boston and especially the central city of Boston, what we have to say applies to other metropolitan areas and their central cities. The characteristic problems of the large central cities have for a long time been moving outward (without of course leaving the central cities) toward the fringes of the metropolitan areas. Boston's troubles are being reproduced in Somerville, New York City's in Yonkers, Chicago's in Evanston, and San Francisco's in Daly City.

Just as the problems of the central cities have been moving outward, so those of the Eastern metropolises have been moving westward along with the geographic center of population. Problems that used to be more or less peculiar to Boston and other Eastern centers are now equally real in Chicago, Detroit, and Omaha, and are almost as real in Denver, Salt Lake City, and Seattle. There are still conspicuous differences between one part of urban America and another, but they are mainly differences of form rather than of kind. In parts of the Southwest where the climate is mild, for example, the slums may be in shanties on the edge of the metropolis rather than in tenement districts in the midst of it.

The American urban condition is in fact spreading over much of the world. In Europe, Japan, Australia, and parts of Latin America our metropolitan areas are being consciously or unconsciously imitated. Thus, although our attention in this book is fixed on Boston and its region, many of the problems—and potentialities—that we discuss are on their way to becoming, if indeed they have not already become, nationwide and even worldwide.

The chapters that follow first appeared in the form of articles published as full-page advertisements in all of the Boston newspapers during the period 1962–1965. These dailies have a circulation of over one and a quarter million. Richard Chapman, then President (now Chairman) of New England Merchants National Bank, conceived the idea of the series. As a business leader who had long been very much involved in efforts to improve the Boston region, he became convinced that a fresh approach to persistent problems, published in a manner that would reach a wide audience, would be a useful public service. The aim of the bank and of the authors alike was to stimulate, among public officials, professional, business, and civic leaders, and citizens generally, discussion of new possibilities for urban development.

Mr. Chapman and two of his colleagues, Frank Christian and Edward Hickey, were helpful critics without in any way infringing our freedom to say what we wished—freedom without which, of course, we could not have proceeded. It is evidence of our independence—and their forbearance—that some of the things we said provoked great outcries against the bank. (Curiously, the one effort to muffle us was made by a newspaper which declined to publish our article on the schools as an advertisement.) We are particularly grateful to Mr. Chapman and his associates for their suggestions and for their confidence in us.

Others who helped us with criticism and information were: Otto Eckstein, Donald Graham, Helen Hughes, Edward Logue, Edmund L. McNamara, Margy Meyerson, Walter Miller, Joseph Slavet, and Joseph Turley. We thank James Q. Wilson for his assistance throughout the undertaking.

The articles appear here in substantially the form in which they were first published. The order of the chapters is slightly different, and we have added a few footnotes to bring certain matters up-to-date.

1 The Power to Govern

Massachusetts meddles in the affairs of its cities more, probably, than does any other state. It is one of fourteen states that make no provision for municipal home rule, and its interference in local matters is more extensive and persistent than that of most, or perhaps all, of the others.

One third of all of the bills considered by the General Court (the state legislature) in four sample years of the past decade dealt with municipal rather than state matters. Of the 1,097 bills dealing with municipal matters that were passed in these four years, 273 placed obligations on the municipalities which they were not free to reject.

Boston is the most interfered-with city in Massachusetts, and probably the most interfered-with in the United States. The Finance Commission, which has power to investigate city affairs, is appointed by the governor. So is the City Licensing Board.* The Zoning Commission, too, operates under the shadow of the state: its regulations are without effect until twelve months after they have been filed with the clerk of the Senate. Even the methods by which Boston obtains tax revenues to pay for its services are dictated by the legislature.

The General Court, which has the final say on most matters affecting Boston, is little disposed to consult with the city's

Note: This chapter was published in the Boston newspapers in late February 1962.

* When this chapter was first published, Boston's police commissioner was appointed by the governor, but in April 1962 the legislature gave the mayor the power to appoint and remove the police commissioner.

2. The Massachusetts Senate, an unusual picture taken in 1965.

elected officials. Every year the mayor of Boston goes hat in hand to the State House to ask for passage of certain bills he thinks are in the city's interest, and every year he returns empty-handed or nearly so. In 1961, for example, Mayor Collins offered twelve Boston bills, of which only two were passed in substantially the form he recommended; his department heads submitted fourteen bills, of which only four were passed. And this poor record — six out of twenty-six — is made poorer by the fact that the bills passed were not the most important ones.

How did Boston get into this situation?

To begin with, one must remember that in the American system of government there is no such thing as an inherent right of local self-government. So far as the United States Constitution is concerned, cities do not exist. It gives certain powers to the federal government, and all other powers it reserves "to the

States respectively, or to the people." Cities and towns are the creations of the states and get all of their powers from them. If a state decided to do so, it could abolish all of its cities.

The supremacy of state over local government is a fixed feature of the American political system. It does not, however, necessitate the harassment of the cities or the interference of the states in matters of purely local concern. To see why it has meant this in Massachusetts, one must go back into history.

The framers of the Massachusetts constitution believed that in order to guarantee civil liberty it was essential to give every citizen the right to place any grievance before the General Court. Article XIV of the Declaration of Rights guarantees the right of the citizen to petition the legislature. In effect, this brings any matter at all, no matter how local in character it may be, potentially within the reach of the state.

Although it began as a protection to civil liberty, state interference in local affairs came to have a very different function. Toward the end of the last century, when Irish immigrants became numerous enough to elect a mayor of Boston, the Yankees who until then had run the city saw some obvious advantages in state control of it. The state electorate was still rural, Yankee, and Republican and would remain so for a long time to come. By moving from the City Hall to the State House, the Yankees could keep a good deal of their control, despite the voters of Boston.

Today, of course, no one thinks that the maintenance of civil liberty depends upon the right of the individual to petition the legislature. And the Yankees and Republicans — those of them who are still around — no longer imagine that they alone are capable of running the city or that, even if they were, they could do so from the State House. Nowadays the state electorate is not so very different from the Boston one. Democrats took control of the House in 1948 and of the Senate in 1958 (a year in which they controlled both houses and the governorship). Under the circumstances, the partisan advantage in keeping Boston under the thumb of the legislature had ceased to exist.

The circumstances having changed, why not give Boston a greater measure of home rule?

Many people favor doing that. The mayor of Boston has urged

it in very strong terms. So have many businessmen and other civic leaders. Since the Second World War, twenty-seven home rule proposals have been introduced into the General Court. Only one was enacted into law. (This was the Home Rule Act of 1951, which increased the powers of the cities somewhat.) Neither this law nor the several measures still under consideration will change the situation fundamentally, however.

Those who support home rule generally do so on the grounds that it is more democratic. Putting power over local affairs in the hands of the local government is, they say, a way of giving the people of the locality a better opportunity to decide matters for themselves. They think of control by the legislature as being "outside control." Control by local government, they say, is control "by the people."

There is a good deal of truth in this view. But — paradoxical as it may seem — there is as much, perhaps even more, truth in the opposite view. For the fact is that when the legislature interferes in Boston's affairs it does so, almost always, at the behest of interests that exist within Boston. In short, city interests find it easier to get their way by going to the State House than by going to the City Hall.

This, for example, is what the Boston firemen did in 1958. When the mayor and city council refused to raise their pay, the firemen got the legislature to put the question before the voters in a referendum. The pay raise was overwhelmingly approved.*

This shows that the case for home rule is not simply one of "local democracy" as against "rule by outsiders." And it raises the question whether the cities, if they had the final say, would not be subject to the very same pressures that the legislature now is. Perhaps they would be even less able than the legislature to resist those pressures.

Another crucial question must also be faced by the advocates of home rule. If the cities are made truly independent, will not their independence stand in the way of joint action in matters that are of metropolitan importance?

The concept of municipal home rule was formed at a time when cities were geographically separate and to a large extent economically independent of each other. Now one city runs into

* The voters approved a pay raise for the policemen under similar circumstances in 1964.

another; people live in one city and work in another, and there are few important public works that do not involve several cities at least. Transportation, water supply and sewage disposal, industrial development, the relocation aspects of urban renewal, and the administration of taxation—these are all functions that cannot be carried on, or cannot be efficiently carried on, except on a metropolitan, or at least an inter-city, basis.

If the cities all have a high degree of home rule, it will be for all practical purposes impossible to deal effectively with these important problems. Obviously the ideal solution would be to sort out the more-than-local functions from the purely local ones, and then to give the cities a high degree of home rule with respect to the latter only. But this is easier said than done. It is not possible to draw lines of this kind except on a case-by-case basis. No one could possibly write a law which distinguishes usefully between what is "purely local" and what is not.

On balance, we think that the present system, despite its defects, is better than the alternative of total home rule. To the extent that it had any effect at all, changing the basic legal relation of the city to the state might very well make matters worse instead of better.

More can be accomplished, we think, by improving the organization of city governments than by redefining their powers. Boston, for example, is run by many local governments rather than by one. The mayor and the city council have little power to influence directly the affairs of the School Committee, the Redevelopment Authority, and several other such bodies. Although the mayor appoints the members of the Redevelopment Authority, he cannot remove them except for cause and after public hearings, which means, for all practical purposes, that he cannot remove them at all.

Because he does not have the authority to tell such bodies what to do, the mayor must spend a great part of his time trying to persuade them or to entice them. Often enough he does not succeed, and they go their own ways without coordination. Since Boston, a nonpartisan city, is not governed by political parties, the mayor has few if any political favors to offer. It is therefore much harder for him to secure the cooperation he needs than it is for most big-city mayors.

Even with regard to the departments under his direct control, the mayor is hedged about with restrictions. He cannot fire incompetent employees. He cannot transfer money from a department where it is not needed to one where it is needed. Sometimes he cannot tell a department head what policy he is to follow.

There was a time when the business of a city like Boston was uncomplicated enough to allow this kind of thing. Today it is not. Today the management of a large city requires a high degree of centralization.

There was a time, too, when the voters had good cause to distrust the men they elected to office. Keeping the power divided was a necessary precaution. Today, however, the electorate can trust itself to choose mayors who are honest, able, and dedicated.

We believe that Boston requires strong leadership, and that the mayor is the one man in a position to give it. We ought, then, to give the mayor the authority he needs to do the job well. Specifically, we ought to give him authority over all city functions and authority to appoint and to remove at will all of his principal subordinates, and authority to hire and fire and to fix the terms of employment of all city employees.

If all this were done, nothing the General Court might do would prevent Boston from being the best-governed city in the nation.

2 The City and the Suburbs

The United States used to be a nation of farms and villages. Then it became one of cities and towns. Now it is one of metropolises.

One hundred and thirteen million people—three out of five Americans—live in 212 metropolitan areas. Within Massachusetts there are eight such areas with 100,000 or more population, the largest of which (as defined by the Census) includes Boston, the rest of Suffolk county, and parts of Essex, Middlesex, Norfolk and Plymouth counties. Four out of five Massachusetts people live in the metropolitan areas.

Hand-me-down governmental structure exists in all metropolitan areas. Whether it can stand the shock of the sudden population growth is a serious question. Many well-informed people think that it cannot. Metropolitan organization, they say, is already a grave problem, and it is getting steadily worse.

A metropolitan area is a cluster of one or more central cities and their adjacent suburbs; the cluster gets its unity from geography and from economic connections, not from a common legal boundary. To an observer from the air, a metropolitan area looks like a single city or municipality. It is not governed as one, however. Hence "the problem of metropolitan organization."

Looked at closely, this turns out to be two quite separate and distinct problems.

One is waste and confusion, which arise, presumably, from the presence of a large number of governmental jurisdictions

Note: This chapter was published in the Boston newspapers in late March 1962.

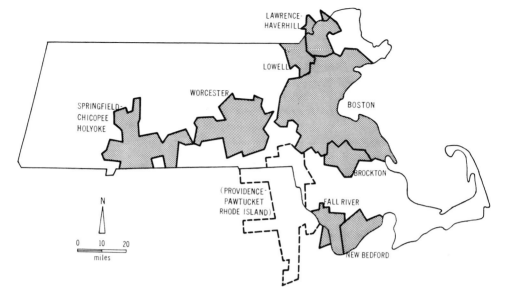

N

0   10   20

miles

METROPOLITAN MASSACHUSETTS: the eight Standard Metropolitan Statistical Areas with 100,000 or more population (Source: U. S. Census of Population, 1960, Massachusetts)

within a single area. In the Boston metropolitan area, for example, there are, in addition to the five county governments, seventeen city governments, fifty-nine town governments, some regional school districts and other special-function districts.*

The other problem arises from the absence of any general-purpose government that can plan and act in a coordinated way with regard to all of the matters that must be treated on an area-wide, rather than a city-wide, basis.

Nowhere in the United States is there a government that has general jurisdiction over the whole of a metropolitan area.

Certainly the mere fact that there are numerous governments in one place is not in itself evidence of waste and confusion. People do not object to having many independent colleges, or banks, or grocery stores in a single place. Why should it be as-

The City and the Suburbs

18

---

* A good example of a special-function district is the Massachusetts Bay Transportation Authority (MBTA), which replaced another special-function district, the Metropolitan Transit Authority (MTA), in June 1964. The new agency was given jurisdiction in an area including seventy-eight cities and towns and wide powers to enter into contracts with private rail and bus transportation companies. The MTA had been serving fourteen cities and towns.

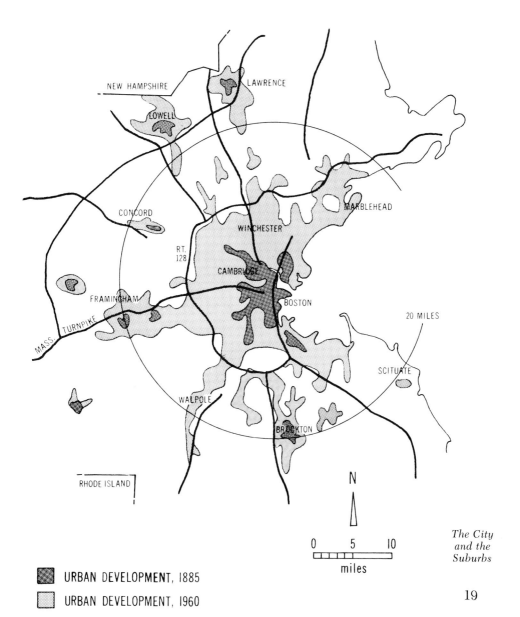

NEW HAMPSHIRE

LAWRENCE

LOWELL

CONCORD

MARBLEHEAD

WINCHESTER

RT.
128

CAMBRIDGE

FRAMINGHAM

BOSTON

20 MILES

MASS. TURNPIKE

SCITUATE

WALPOLE

BROCKTON

RHODE ISLAND

N

0   5   10

miles

URBAN DEVELOPMENT, 1885

URBAN DEVELOPMENT, 1960

EXPRESSWAYS, BUILT AND UNDER CONSTRUCTION

BOSTON REGION: urban development, 1885 and 1960 (Source:
Massachusetts Mass Transportation Commission, Boston Regional
Survey, 1963)

sumed that there are not also advantages in having independent local governments?

Many suppose that it would cost less to operate the cities if numerous small ones were merged into a single big one. Everyone knows that there are often economies to be had from large-scale organization. There is evidence, however, that many cities and some towns are already large enough to operate economically. The people who have studied the question most carefully point out that there is a level beyond which any increase in size may be accompanied by a decrease in efficiency.

But even if sizable savings could be had from consolidating cities and towns, it would not necessarily follow that it would generally be desirable to consolidate them. Many people take great satisfaction from feeling that their local government is close to them. Their feeling may be ill-founded, or they may be foolish to attach so much importance to it. We do not happen to think so. In any case, people's tastes in such matters — whether well-founded or not — are entitled to a good deal of weight. If people are willing to pay what it may cost to enjoy the feeling that local government is close to them, they should have the opportunity.

Sometimes small, separate municipal governments are objected to on the grounds that they produce inequalities in service levels. One town, for example, may have excellent snow removal and street cleaning while a nearby one has very poor snow removal and street cleaning. Only metropolitan government, it is said, can remedy such inequalities.

We do not think that inequalities of this sort are necessarily undesirable and may even be a good thing. Provided every community meets a certain minimum level of health, safety, and welfare, there is much to be said for letting people decide locally how much of each service they wish to pay for and consume. If the people of one community want to economize on street lighting and sidewalks and the people of another community want to splurge on them, each should be able to do so.

Consumers of local government services should have a wide range of choice for the same reasons that consumers of anything from books to cars should have a choice.

There are some local government problems that involve two

or three municipalities. These require intergovernmental co-operation, but not necessarily metropolitan organization. Many cities have numerous formal and informal cooperative arrange-ments with neighboring cities and with governmental bodies; such arrangements can easily be extended to new situations as need arises. Suburbs, for example, may contract with a large city to purchase fire protection (as some municipalities in this area already do), police laboratory work, or other services that they cannot economically organize for themselves.

There would be more such cooperative arrangements if the state legislatures, including ours in Massachusetts, encouraged them by making it easy for local governments to buy and sell services from each other whenever doing so was mutually ad-vantageous. Where legislatures stand in the way of such cooper-ation, the reason is usually political: some interest thinks it would be better served if the cooperation did not take place. Pressures from special interests would continue, of course, even if there were metropolitan government. Politics would not go out just because metropolitan government came in.

Some functions, however, cannot be well performed except on a metropolitan basis. In most places these are:

1. *Transportation.* The routing of major highways, the loca-tion of major truck terminals, and measures to deal with the commuter's automobile, commuter railroads and mass transit — these cannot advantageously be left to the separate cities. For these a metropolitan design is essential.

2. *Real estate taxation.* Some communities can provide high levels of service while charging low taxes because they are lucky enough to have industry or other valuable property within their borders. Other communities, not so fortunate in their tax bases, must provide inferior services while charging high taxes.

Such inequities are inherently undesirable. They are espe-cially so when, as often happens, they impel municipalities to compete to attract industry and, sometimes, to discourage the settlement of low-income families who, because they often have many children in school, will cost the local government·more in services than they will pay to it in taxes. From the standpoint of the metropolitan area as a whole, such competition is detrimental. We plan to return to these matters in another chapter.

3. *Water supply and sewage disposal.* The principal facilities of this kind should be designed and operated on a metropolitan basis, as is done in the Boston area by the Metropolitan District Commission (MDC). This is necessary because the wastes from one community are likely to endanger the health of other communities and because there are large economies to be had by putting water storage and treatment facilities on an inter-city basis.

4. *Air pollution control.* Because a nuisance or threat to public health generated in one place may make itself felt in another, air pollution control measures are not likely to be effective unless they are applied on a metropolitan basis.

5. *Major outdoor recreation areas.* If large tracts of open space are to be preserved for the enjoyment of all the people of a metropolitan area, responsibility for buying, developing, and managing the land must be in the hands of a body able to plan for the needs of the area as a whole. (Small parks and playgrounds are an entirely different matter since they are intended to serve only the people of one city, town, or residential district.)

Many people feel that the final solution to the problem of metropolitan organization must be the establishment of a government having area-wide jurisdiction over all these functions and perhaps others as well. Plans to establish such governments have been put forward in more than one hundred places in the last half century. In practically all cases, they have come to nothing because of political opposition.

As a rule, Democratic leaders in the central cities do not like having large numbers of suburbanites, many of whom are Republican, added to their municipalities. Nor do Republican leaders in the outlying areas usually want their municipalities added to the central cities; they like it better, naturally, to have a high proportion of Republicans.

The politicians are not the only opponents of metropolitan government, of course. Between the people who live in the central cities and those who live in the suburbs there are many differences of opinion and interest. When plans for consolidation of governments have been put before electorates, they have almost always been voted down.

Boston, although nonpartisan in city elections, is no exception to the general rule. Given the politics of the Boston region, there is little chance of creating a supergovernment for this metropolitan area in the foreseeable future.

The forms of organization that have proved most acceptable in the United States are the special-function districts and authorities. These are public corporations set up to do one thing, or, sometimes (as in the case of MDC, which provides water, sewage disposal, and recreation facilities) two or three things on a more-than-local basis. In the last ten years the number of such districts or authorities in the United States has increased spectacularly. (The MDC, incidentally, has been a model for the establishment of special districts in several metropolitan regions.)

Two objections are often made to these forms of organization.

One is that they are not responsive to popular control. Usually the heads of the agencies are appointed rather than elected, and sometimes they do not have to go to the legislature for appropriations. Having so much freedom of action, they are often very effective in doing their job. But they are apt to be high-handed and to forget that their job is to do what the public wants done, not what the administrators want to do.

The other objection that is made to the special district or authority is that since it has jurisdiction over only one (or at any rate very few) functions, it is wholly unable to deal with a most fundamental problem, that of coordinating the related functions of government within the metropolitan area.

We believe that the best that can be done in the Boston metropolitan area is to improve such organization as we already have. This is not just a matter of making a virtue of necessity. In our judgment, the existing organization is potentially well suited to cope with the problems that are really of metropolitan importance.

Some of the functions which must be performed on a metropolitan-area basis are now being performed by the state government and by special districts organized by it. In Chapter 1 we pointed out that far-reaching home rule for cities would make it difficult or impossible for the state, or any other governmental body, to deal effectively with metropolitan problems.

The governor should be the chief executive in metropolitan-area matters — but not in purely municipal matters — both for the

Boston area and for all of Massachusetts. In order to be effective in this, he should have more legal and political power than he has at present. He should have a four-year term of office; he should have such power to hire and fire as would give him great strength in dealing with the legislature; he should be free of encumbrances like the Executive Council; he should have in his office a staff of senior civil servants qualified to handle metropolitan activities; and he should have the advice of metropolitan planning councils in each urban area.* If they worked closely with the governor and his technical staff, such planning councils might have great influence.

The objectionable features of the special-district or authority form of organization—its unresponsiveness to popular control and its inability to bring about coordination—can be overcome by making such agencies responsible to the governor. This could be done by giving him the power to appoint and to remove at will a majority of the commissioners of such bodies.

When one remembers that four out of five Massachusetts people already live in metropolitan areas and that the proportion who live in them is bound to increase, it is hard to see how the Commonwealth can fail to become the equivalent, for all practical purposes, of eight or more metropolitan governments.

That Massachusetts is small enough to allow this may prove a great blessing. It may mean that metropolitan government and planning, in fact if not in name, will come into being here sooner than it will elsewhere.

* In a referendum in 1964, the governor's term of office was extended to four years, beginning in 1966. The statutory powers of the Executive Council were sharply curtailed.

3 The Tax Tangle

Boston is in a tough financial squeeze—the worst, perhaps, of any large city in the United States.

The per capita cost of local government here is nearly $300. That is more than in any city of comparable size anywhere in the country.

The Boston property tax rate is also higher than any other. Some investors think that it is confiscatory. That may be why the city did not develop more in the past generation.

The city's debt is about 10 percent of its actual property values. Many well-informed people feel that it cannot safely go higher unless the economic position of the city improves greatly.

Boston's record between 1950 and 1960, however, was better than that of most cities. In the United States as a whole, the per capita cost of local government increased by 100 percent in this period. In Boston it increased by 63 percent.

Past waste and extravagance account for much of the city's predicament, but the mayor of Boston has committed his administration to eliminate the unnecessary and he has shown that he means what he says. There is still room for improvement, of course, but much has been achieved in a short time. The efficiency of the city government is increasing at an encouraging rate.

Despite these increases in efficiency, the signs point to further rises in the cost of local government.

Note: This chapter was published in the Boston newspapers in April 1962.

One reason for this is that the prices of the things that city governments buy have been increasing. In the United States as a whole, these price increases account for about one third of the increase in the cost of local government.

Inflation has hit city governments even harder than it has hit people. This is because the things that city governments buy — especially equipment and services — have gone up in price faster than have groceries, rents, and other things that ordinary consumers buy.

City salaries, for example, have been going up steadily all over the country, and these account for about 40 percent of all local-government spending. We think these increases are entirely justified for some public services — teachers, for example. For many municipal functions, however, there can well be fewer jobs but better-paid ones.

Another reason why the cost of local government has gone up is that many people have moved to new suburbs. This has not only made necessary the building of many schools, roads, and other facilities in these communities but also added to the financial troubles of the central cities. Boston, for example, provides a good many services for the growing number of suburbanites who come into the city to work and to shop. At the same time its ability to raise revenue has been impaired by the movement of a good many of its more prosperous residents to the suburbs.

Like most central cities, Boston has more than its share of the metropolitan area's low-income families and less than its share of the well-to-do. That means double trouble financially, for the poorer the family, the more local-government service it requires and the less it is able to contribute in taxes.

The most important reason for the steady rise in the cost of local government, however, is that the ordinary citizen wants more and better city services than before. He wants better schools, better police protection, better parking facilities, and so on.

This is a good thing. People should want better schools, better police protection, and all the rest. And if people want them, it is up to local government to supply them. That (among other things) is what democracy is all about.

If local government does not respond adequately to the needs and wishes of its citizens it will probably be pushed into the background by the federal government. That would be undesirable. The federal government already has more on its hands than it can tend to properly.

No doubt further increases in the cost of local government are inevitable. Like it or not, then, the taxpayer is going to have to bear heavier burdens. That makes this an appropriate time to consider some of the fundamentals of tax policy.

We would like to suggest five general standards as the basis for a good local tax system.

1. *The system should be fair and equitable.* No one class of taxpayers—homeowners, for example—should bear an undue share of the burden, and within each category of taxpayer every individual should pay the same tax as every other who is similarly situated. All persons owning homes of the same value should pay the same tax on them, for example.

2. *The tax should encourage honesty* on the part of taxpayers and it should be cheap and simple to administer.

3. *The tax should stimulate the economic growth* and prosperity of the city, or at any rate it should impede it as little as possible. No matter what virtues it may have in other respects, a tax that discourages investment and in this way reduces the income of the community is a bad tax.

4. *The tax should serve as an indication of citizens' demand for local government services.* Only as we know how much taxes a citizen is willing to pay or what services he is willing to forego for the sake of getting a specific city service like better streets, can we judge how much he really wants that service. He wants the best possible streets of course—if somebody else is going to pay for them. But if he is going to pay for them himself, he may want streets that are something less than the best possible. Which of these "wants" ought to be taken most seriously? We think the latter.

5. *Finally, a good tax system must be politically workable.* We mean by this that the elected officials should be able to raise the revenues that are required without exposing themselves to undue political hazards in the process. We say this not necessarily because we want to make life pleasanter for politicians,

but because we think that if the political hazards of raising it are excessive the revenue that is needed will never be raised.

The personal property tax on movable goods should be abolished. Property that is not visible either escapes taxation altogether or else is taxed capriciously. The personal property tax does not meet any of the standards we listed and it has no virtues at all.

The real property tax (on land and buildings) produces a fairly stable return, is easy to administer (although hard to administer *well*), and over the years it has come to have a high degree of political acceptability. On the other hand, it is not very equitable: it hits some elements of the population harder than it does others and, the difficulty of making accurate assessments being great, there are always injustices in its operation.

But the most serious defect of the real property tax is that it discourages new investment. As it stands, the tax offers property owners no incentive to tear down old houses, office buildings, stores, and factories and build better ones in their places. On the contrary, it actually penalizes efforts at modernization; a new building is at a tax disadvantage as compared to an old one.

In a city like Boston, which has so many obsolete buildings, a tax system that works this way cannot be defended.

The situation would not be so bad if Boston's tax rate were based upon the income-producing value of real estate rather than upon its market value. If this were the case, slum owners, for example, would no longer get a free ride. They are getting one now because their properties have low values despite their high returns. This being the case, the slum owner pays little in taxes although he puts the city to much expense.

As the law stands, assessors cannot go very far in taking the income return of a property into account.

The best way to remove the inhibiting effect of the property tax, however, would be to tax the land component of real estate relatively heavily and the building component relatively lightly. A tax on land is normally capitalized (that is, the price of the land changes to take the tax into account) while one on buildings is (except in a depression) normally passed on to tenants.

By taxing land heavily and buildings lightly the city would

give owners an incentive to build on their land if it is vacant or to rebuild on it if it is already built upon, or else to sell it to someone who would build on it.* In this way more might be accomplished in the elimination of slums and blighted areas than is likely to be accomplished by federally aided housing and renewal programs.

Local governments should make the widest possible use of fee-for-service charges. Boston, like most cities, charges the user for some services. The national trend is toward extending the use of such charges. There are limits, of course, beyond which it is neither practical nor desirable to go. No one, for example, would exclude children from public schools because their parents cannot pay the school bill. But when all such necessary exceptions have been made, there are many opportunities to apply the principle that the user should pay for what he gets. In recreation, transportation, and some other facilities this is probably the only way that the demand for service can be kept from skyrocketing.

Whatever else may be done or not done, the legislature should give Boston wide latitude to choose its tax sources.

At present it has less latitude than other large cities. The others can tax what people earn and what they spend as well as what they own. Boston is tied to the property tax. The legislature should set it free.

Boston and the other cities of the Commonwealth — once they get their freedom — should diversify their tax sources. Using a sales or payroll tax, for example, along with the property tax, they can avoid putting an unfair tax burden on any class of taxpayer. If the cities act together in diversifying their sources of revenue as we believe they would, these taxes could best be administered for the cities by the state.

By diversifying, Boston can capture revenue that now escapes it entirely. About one third of the property in Boston is exempt from taxation. (This is a bigger proportion, incidentally, than in any other large city except Washington, D.C.) With the availa-

* If we were writing this today, we would still emphasize the importance of a differential tax for land and buildings but would point out that the decision as to which component to tax more heavily ought to be based on the strategy of the locality. For example, does it choose to encourage or slow down new development?

bility of sales or payroll taxes, the city could make up for this loss without injury to the many church, hospital, educational, and governmental institutions that play so vital a part in the life of the city.

As we said in Chapter 2, we believe that the administration and planning of *certain* functions should be performed by the state on a metropolitan area-wide basis. One of the things that the state might do is to assess property and collect taxes, turning the revenue over to local governments to spend. The state would establish a basic tax rate sufficient to provide adequate levels of service throughout the metropolitan area. Those localities wanting to provide themselves with more than this minimum-adequate level of service could levy an additional tax which the state would collect for them.

The advantage of this arrangement would be the elimination of the inequalities that exist in the tax bases of the localities and, consequently, the elimination also of *harmful* competition among them for industries and other tax "plums" within a metropolitan area.

There are those who think that unless the state spends in Boston (or gives to Boston to spend) an amount equal to what it collects in Boston, the people of the city are short-changed.

The mayor of Boston has made it clear that he feels that the city is being unfairly treated because the state collects tens of millions a year more from the city than it returns to it.

We think that an elected official ought to speak up for his constituents as loudly as he can. It is not at all clear to us, however, that the state should return to a locality *exactly* what it collects in it. If this principle were applied to the federal government, an enormous amount would be returned to Manhattan and none could be transferred from Manhattan to any less highly developed area.

The proper relation between what the state collects in a locality and what it returns to that locality cannot, we think, be derived from any simple formula. No one should be discriminated against for living in Boston — that much is sure. But this does not necessarily mean that some of the revenue raised in Boston should not be spent elsewhere.

No matter what taxes are levied or what level of government levies them, the moderate-income group is going to have to pay about the same share—a very large share, that is—of the total tax bill. This is bound to be the case, for the simple reason that moderate-income people are by far the most numerous.

Any future tax bill is going to be awfully hard to swallow. But we had better get prepared to do so because we have little choice.

4 Traffic and Transit

Nobody is happy now with Boston's transportation. Motorists complain of traffic snarls and lack of parking. Transit commuters complain of poor service. Railroad commuters on abandoned lines complain of no service. Businessmen in transportation complain of the money they lose. Public officials despair. Yet Boston is one of the few areas in the country which has all of the most important elements that must go into a good transportation system.

Boston Has Good Transit. It is one of the four cities in America lucky enough to have a subway system (the others are New York, Philadelphia, and Chicago) and one of the few with good streetcar lines. Its transit lines are well designed (a few cities have begun to take seriously the recommendation that transit lines be put on median strips along expressways, but Boston has run its streetcars this way on Commonwealth Avenue for many years), and the subway and elevated lines carry a large number of people from downtown to many of the nearby suburbs at relatively low cost.

Boston Has Good Highways. The first major circumferential highway to be built around any large metropolis was built around Boston. Most cities run their expressways out from the center only, but Boston's ring road, Route 128, connects with radials in such a way as to create a commercial and industrial belt that is easily accessible to the whole metropolitan area.

Note: This chapter was published in the Boston newspapers in September 1962.

3. Traffic in Kenmore Square at 4:45 p.m., looking approximately east-ward along Beacon Street (left) and Commonwealth Avenue.

Boston Has Room for Parking Places. To be sure, there is still a shortage of parking in downtown Boston. But Boston, unlike many central cities, has spread out enough in recent years to make possible the creation of many more parking places where they are needed. The business core of most cities is so compact that as a practical matter it is impossible to provide adequate parking within easy walking distance of the places to which most people want to go. Luckily for Boston, its inner core extending into Back Bay is not so heavily built up that additional sites cannot be turned into parking facilities.

The Massachusetts Mass Transportation Commission is about to take a long, hard ($10,200,000) look at the passenger transportation problem in the Boston region and other cities in the Commonwealth.*

The answers that one finds in such studies depend upon the questions that one asks. What is needed to begin with is a point of view that will lead to the right questions.

We think a new transportation policy for the Boston area should be based upon three general principles:

First, its object should be to give consumers what they want — that is, whatever they are ready and willing to pay for. The primary objective should not be to use the transportation system as a device for remaking the character of the city to suit the image of some one group or interest. If people want to ride in automobiles rather than on subways, policy should respect their wishes so far as possible. It should not impose upon them the tastes of others — whether they be downtown merchants or transit officials or any other special group.

Second, the user should be charged for his use of transportation facilities. If consumers want expressways, they should have them but they should pay their share of the costs either in the form of tolls or as direct taxes. Otherwise, they will want highways to get them from their homes to their workplaces, without delay and with guaranteed parking, regardless of the costs to others. Similarly, if rapid-transit riders want air-conditioned cars, they should have them, but they should pay the added costs in higher fares. The justification for charging the user for the benefits he receives is not justice alone (although that enters into it), but the impossibility of finding out in any other way what it is that consumers really want. We cannot find out simply by asking what they want in the way of transportation or other goods and

* The Mass Transportation Commission used $5.4 million to finance a variety of experiments on service improvement and fare reduction, and it allocated $4.8 million to the Boston Regional Planning Program. In 1964 the commission's functions were transferred to the Department of Commerce and Development.

services. We must present alternatives in such a way that we can learn what consumers are willing to give up in time or money or something else they value in order to get what they say they want.

Third, it should look for the best combination of devices or measures or technologies and not for any one that represents "the solution." Although we have spoken above of "the consumer," actually there are various groups of consumers, each with different requirements. Not all consumers will be served by better rapid transit. Or by better highways. Or by more parking. It is by putting these and other elements together effectively that we will get the best results. This best "package" approach may leave some elements of the combination—for example, parking—in a less-than-optimum condition. But it is the combination, not the separate elements, that should be optimum.

The problem of the Boston metropolitan area is to provide for the changing character of its consumers and at the same time to make the best possible use of its present advantages. For this it needs a general strategy to coordinate the different kinds of passenger transportation. As we wrote in Chapter 2, transportation should be planned on a metropolitan-wide basis, and the state is the best means for doing so.

A general strategy for transportation must be based on up-to-date notions of what the city is like, and of what transportation technology is like. The forms of cities change when a new kind of transportation is developed. The use of cars and trucks, for example, radically altered the use of the city. When people and goods were hauled on rails, downtown was the most desirable place to locate stores, offices, light industries and other economic activities, because downtown was the center for converging transit and rail lines. As highways were built and the number of cars increased, however, most sections of the metropolitan area became reasonably accessible for commerce, industry, and public uses as well as for housing. Downtown declined.

Many people assume that a declining downtown can be restored by restoring the kind of transportation that existed before the decline set in. They think that rapid-transit systems should be built or improved or subsidized to the point where they will drive most of the automobile traffic off the city streets. They assume also that the decline of the downtown has been worst in those cities which do not have good subway or other rail transit systems. Actually, cities without rail transit systems have not suffered any worse decline than have cities with them. Having a good transit system has not guaranteed its use, as witnessed by the decline in the number of riders on Boston's transit system from roughly 400 million in 1946 to 200 million in 1960. To us, this suggests that improvements in the transit system would not guarantee a substantial shift in transportation habits, unless the improved system were vastly more elaborate than anything developed up to now. Such an elaborate system would probably cost much more than it would return in benefits. A major task of a transportation study will be to figure out the costs and benefits of any proposed transportation scheme.

As we see them, the critical elements of the situation, for the present and for the next ten to fifteen years, are these:

The main function of the rapid-transit system is, and will continue to be, the transportation to and from work of the relatively low-income people who live in Boston and the older suburbs. These people ride the transit system to save money. Some of them do not own cars; in many cases the car is used by other members of the family.

Another function of rapid transit — a secondary one — is to carry middle-income shoppers and commuters on those occasions when driving is inconvenient or impossible. As a general rule, middle-income people prefer to drive their cars rather than to take public transportation. But if there is a snowstorm, or if downtown is clogged with Christmas shoppers, the motorist turns to rapid transit for a few days. From the standpoint of this group of users, the rapid-transit system exists as standby service.

A third function of mass rail transportation is to carry a relatively few "exurbanites" to and from their downtown offices. These people ride commuter trains not to save money but for convenience; they like to get their newspapers and business memoranda read on the way to and from the office.

The transit authorities cannot change this pattern of demand fundamentally. The working people who ride the transit system will continue to do so, even if the fare is increased. The middle-

4. A future rapid-transit train. This 1965 photograph shows a full-scale model of the computerized cars to be used in the San Francisco Bay area. An attendant riding in the detachable forward pod will exercise control if necessary, but normally the trains will be operated automatically from a central computer.

income shoppers and commuters will not leave their cars at home and switch to public transportation as a regular thing no matter how cheap the fare. And the few "exurbanites" will commute by train, so long as the trip is more agreeable by train than by car.

There are certain political realities that should be taken into account also. The lower-income people who use the transit system regularly are numerous, but they are not apt to make themselves heard: generally speaking, they do not write editorials, pass resolutions, and testify before legislative committees. There is no "rapid-transit user's lobby" representing these people. On the other hand there are several powerful pressure groups which oppose public subsidies for rapid transit and favor them for highways and parking facilities. The middle-income motorists who use their cars for shopping and commuting are both numerous and politically active.

The "exurbanite" commuters, although influential as individuals, are, of course, too few to be of much account politically.

The most important change in the composition of these groups in the next decade probably will be in the size and composition of the regular users of public transportation. As the national income rises, more and more people will join the middle-income group and the proportion of middle-income families with more than one car will go up. The central city and the older suburbs will still have a good many people who will not be able to afford —or at any rate, will not own—cars. They will also have a large number of old people—many more than at present—who may find some forms of public transportation more convenient and comfortable than driving.

The number of upper-income commuters will probably increase considerably, as will their average incomes. These people will be able to spend much more for transportation than before, but whether they will be able to keep alive the financially tottering commuter railroads—even after railroad mergers—is questionable.

If this is the situation and the outlook, what does it imply for a general strategy of metropolitan transportation development?

If consumers were obligated to choose transportation on the same pay-for-what-you-get basis as they choose food, we expect that the general pattern of transportation use in metropolitan Boston would not be drastically changed. But there would be many important improvements in service and some new facilities would be added because, we think, people acting as "consumers" are generally willing to support community facilities at a higher level than they are when acting as "voters."

We suspect that if they were given the opportunity, most of the regular riders would be glad to pay somewhat higher fares in order to get such improvements as air-conditioned cars, whereas the middle-income shoppers and commuters who make only occasional use of public transportation are not likely to be willing to pay very much in added taxes to have it improved. However, these middle-income groups may be willing to pay for transit extension to unserved areas to satisfy their desire for

5. Fairground-type motor train loads up at a parking area in Disneyland. This and other devices have possible application to the Boston area.

transit standby service. These middle-income shoppers and commuters would probably be willing to spend more than they do now to enjoy the freedom and privacy of their cars.

In devising a combination of measures for improved traffic and transit in the Boston area, here are some ideas which are being discussed (and in some cases tried) in cities around the country today:

Separate freight, passenger, and pedestrian traffic in the busiest parts of the central city and in the major access routes.

Remove restrictions on licensing taxis (as in Washington, D.C.) so that many more will be available and at lower fares. Do the same for small, privately owned buses.

6. Minibus in Washington, D.C., serving downtown stores, hotels, and parking areas.

Encourage the use of small cars by taxing cars according to the parking space that they require rather than, as at present, according to their value.

Zone downtown so that wholesalers who store goods will be under some pressure to move their inventories and their trucks—but not their showrooms—out of downtown.

Stagger hours for the use of trucks downtown so that trucks interfere as little as possible with commuter traffic.

Stagger work hours in the city to reduce traffic peaks.

Close some streets and convert them to pedestrian malls.

Where pedestrian malls are used, provide Disneyland or fairground-type vehicles—small enough and slow enough to be used safely among pedestrians—to enable the young and the old and the heavily laden to get from place to place.

Use such vehicles to link parking facilities on the edge of the central business district with key points within the district.

Use hydrofoil, hovercraft or other fast boat service (for example, to connect Boston with its north and south shores and to go up and down the Charles River).

7. Thirty-foot hydrofoil boat skimming the surface of San Francisco Bay.

8. Hovercraft riding on air cushion four feet thick. This Jet Skimmer, operated on a regular schedule by SFO Helicopter Airlines, Inc., carries passengers twenty miles across San Francisco Bay in sixteen minutes. Air forced downward by a fan holds it above the water, and a conventional propeller moves it forward.

Establish a heliport to permit luxury commuting from distant suburbs to the central city.

Provide convenient compounds for picking up and dropping rental cars to encourage their use within the metropolitan area. This will reduce the number of cars on the road.

Use closed-circuit TV and other new communications and data-processing devices to regulate and speed the flow of traffic on the existing highways.

Give buses special lanes on main expressways and priority of access into all expressways.

Establish a permanent state agency to deal not with the parking problem or the transit problem, but with the entire transportation system of metropolitan areas.*

No one should suppose that any combination of the above or other measures or policies will "solve" Boston's problem of congestion.

Any place to which a great many people go at any one time is necessarily congested. The more effective the measures we take to reduce congestion, the more attractive the area will be and the greater the number of people who will therefore go to it. Relief of congestion can be only temporary.

This is not to say that efforts to improve transportation are futile. Quite the contrary. Giving as many people as possible the opportunity to come together in one place at one time is the purpose of a good city transportation system, and, for that matter, of a city.

The more people who can come to Boston the better. If that be congestion, then let us make the most of it!

* The Massachusetts Bay Transportation Authority (MBTA) now has this responsibility for the Boston area.

5 Freight

Boston people do not fume about freight transportation the way they do about the transportation of people. They should. Inefficient and obsolete freight transportation means fewer jobs, lower wages, and smaller profits throughout the Boston metropolitan area. In the long run, the quality of the freight transportation system has a great deal to do with Boston's quality as a community.

Right now our freight transportation is bad. That people are not writing letters to the editor to complain about it does not mean that they have no cause for complaint. They do. Something ought to be done to improve matters—and soon.

The trouble is not with Boston but with the rest of the country. It has been moving steadily away from Boston for more than a century. Population, industry, and purchasing power have moved west and south, leaving us perched here on the edge of the country.

Some coastal cities—Philadelphia, for example—serve extensive and rich tributary areas. Others—like Seattle—do not compete with nearby ports. Boston's area is small and relatively poor. And Boston has many rival ports to contend with. What's more, as New England industry turns to lighter products and to services, the volume of freight it provides is shrinking.

Because of New England's geography and industrial structure, a considerable part of its freight business consists of short-haul and small-unit shipments. The obsolete system of rate regulation

Note: This chapter was published in the Boston newspapers in October 1962.

and other causes make these shipments relatively unprofitable to carriers of all kinds.

To make matters worse, Boston is cluttered with obsolete transportation facilities. These are hand-me-downs from earlier days—a penalty our region pays for having been developed so early.

All this adds up to a rather gloomy picture.

Before trying to decide what measures will improve the situation, let us take a closer look at each of the forms of freight transportation.

The port once dominated American shipping and was the mainstay of the local economy. Now it handles only a twentieth of the tonnage of shipping that clears the country's coastal ports every year. In proportion to population, the Boston port handles less goods than any other large east coast metropolitan area.

Most of our shipping consists of goods such as grain, scrap, and oil which are low in value in relation to their bulk and which do not generate much employment, either in handling or in later processing. Moving a ton of bulk cargo may contribute as little as $1 or $2 to the community, in wages to workers, payments to bankers, forwarders and others. A ton of high-value cargo would contribute $8 to $12 or more. All ports are anxious to get general cargo. The Port Authority tries to get it for Boston, but so far with little success.

Boston is closer to Europe than other major American ports. One might think this would give it an advantage, but it does not. Most of the exports produced in New England—perhaps 80 percent—are shipped from New York. It is not the time it takes crossing the Atlantic that is important: it is the time and, above all, the cost (in which time is only one element) from the beginning of the journey to the end of it. Being closer to Europe means being farther from those points within the United States which are the beginning or the end of the cargo's journey. If the trip by ship is less, then that by rail or truck (the more expensive forms of transport) is correspondingly greater.

9. Boston's Atlantic Avenue waterfront in February 1965. Where ships once abounded, some docks now are used as parking lots, and the area is scheduled for redevelopment. Boston's shrinking port commerce is carried on mainly in other parts of the harbor.

Our port is also at a disadvantage because so few ships enter and leave it. Shipments sometimes suffer costly delays waiting for passage. To avoid these delays they are often sent to New York. The Boston port is also technologically inefficient. Neither it nor any American port can stand comparison with the better European ones. European ports make extensive use of on-shore cranes and other equipment to speed loading and unloading and to reduce labor costs. Everything is arranged to get ships on their way out of the port as fast as possible. This saving of time in port is of the greatest importance to shippers.

The efficient equipment and arrangement of a port reduces the amount of land required for loading and unloading operations, thus making possible other land uses—for port-related industries, housing, and parks.

(The reasons European ports are more efficient than ours are of interest. One is that most of them were badly damaged in the war and had to be rebuilt. Another is that the tide rises so high—twenty or more feet in some cases—that locks are necessary; space within the lock being at a premium, emphasis is given to a quick turn-around. Labor unions in European ports are not so demanding. And finally, ports and their business are more important to Europeans than to us; for some European economies, they are almost matters of life or death.)

The prospect for the port of Boston is not encouraging. There is talk, for example, of running express "container-ships" between New York and Europe. These would be specially designed to handle cargo packed in standardized containers. This would eliminate the cost of crating, reduce handling costs, make fuller use of space on ships, and virtually eliminate pilferage. If developments such as these occur, Boston may lose what little general cargo it now has.

Freight

Our rail freight service is in the doldrums, too. The New York, New Haven and Hartford Railroad, principal rail freight carrier for the region, is bankrupt; its future is very uncertain. There is no freight yard in the Boston area that is fully integrated with truck terminal and port facilities to simplify transshipment. In fact, there is no truly modern rail freight yard in the Boston area.

In the country as a whole, railroads have been losing freight

10. Piggy-back, a Boston strong point. In the piggy-back yard of the Boston and Maine Railroad, mobile gantry cranes, which were put into operation in 1961, are unloading trailers which will be trucked the rest of the way.

to trucks, pipelines, waterways, and air transport. But the decline of rail freight has been greater here than elsewhere.

The railroads were once great carriers of fuel, especially coal. Oil and gas have cut sharply into the use of coal. New England gets its gas by pipeline; its oil comes by water and is transshipped by pipeline.

The advantage of the railroad is greatest (or its disadvantage least) when a large volume of bulk goods is to be moved a long distance. Railroads can handle goods safely in almost any weather, and they can do so (because wheels on rails are almost frictionless) at a very low expenditure of energy per pound moved. These advantages are largely offset, however, by the huge investment required for terminals. A cargo shipped by rail is actually on the move as little as one third of the time; the rest of the time it waits in a costly yard or terminal.

In at least one thing the New England rail freight people have scored. They were among the first to use the "piggy-back" system, in which truck trailer bodies are trucked to flatcars, carried long distances by train, and then hitched again to trucks for the last lap. This development and others, notably the two-deck automobile carrier, have helped keep Boston's rail freight business alive. But it is barely alive.

It is a good sign, nevertheless, that railroad and other transport executives are now keenly aware of the need to combine transport means in ways that give the shipper the best possible door-to-door service. This problem, and the other problems of the railroads, will not be solved merely by merging companies.

Truck transportation has, in recent years, become the principal means of moving goods in and out of Boston. Since the war, Boston has gained more than most major cities in the United States through truck hauling of certain commodities—fresh fruits and vegetables, for example.

Trucks are well suited for most of our freight needs—to carry foodstuffs and other consumer goods coming in to market, and to carry low-bulk products of Boston's economy out to the rest of the nation.

Express highways have given trucks a special advantage. As more expressways are built, the railroads may lose to the trucks some of the commodities—cement, for example—on which they now depend heavily. Better highways may also hurt Boston's port by making it cheaper to ship to and from the port of New York.

Although the public has more or less unwittingly helped truckers by providing good highways, it has not taken the next logical step, providing those facilities that are needed along with highways. Boston has no union trucking terminal where small packages can be collected into large shipments. We have not set aside a special district, accessible to major highways, where trucking firms can locate their terminals and related facilities. A number of firms have established facilities on or near Route 128, and this is no doubt a good thing. It would have been a better thing, however, if public authorities had taken the lead in making a suitable district available to them.

But progress is being made. Boston is planning to develop a truck terminal and rail, heliport, marina (a harbor for very small boats), and industrial park facilities on a 35-acre site near North Station. Many public agencies and private investors are cooperating in this.*

* These plans fell through.

11. Jet airfreighter at Logan Airport. Cargo is packed into "igloos" which are the shape of the plane's interior and which are moved into the plane on power rollers.

In air freight transport, Boston has a great asset that should be strengthened and improved. In the last ten years, our foreign cargo has increased more than tenfold and our domestic cargo has doubled. Few cities can match this record.

Products made in the Boston area are peculiarly suited to air shipment. The value-per-pound of many of them is very high. In an industry like electronics, the cost of transportation—even expensive transportation—is a relatively unimportant item. For this reason, some firms that buy electronics equipment prefer to order supplies as they need them rather than to maintain warehouses. By stocking supplies for only a few days, a firm can often cut its storage costs by half or more. The saving is frequently more than enough to pay the extra cost of shipping by air.

To take advantage of these opportunities, however, business

firms must learn how to organize their distribution systems for air cargo, the airlines must master the art of containerization and must improve the coordination of air and ground freight handling, and airport managers must learn how to keep cargo on the move. These are matters that private and public groups should study at once. In doing so, they should take into account that air cargo rates will probably be reduced and that the design of cargo planes will be improved.

In the last century, when Boston was out-competed by other parts of the country, enterprising men used their ingenuity to develop the Clipper Ship and with it to open up the China trade. We believe that the air cargo plane can be the Clipper Ship of tomorrow.

There is no use pretending that Boston can regain its place as a big shipper of freight. It does not have enough big industry and it is not close enough to the places that do. Now that the federal courts have put an end to discrimination in rail rates in favor of Southern ports and against Eastern ones, our situation may improve somewhat. In the long run, the shipping business will go where it is cheapest for it to go, and Boston will remain at a disadvantage in many respects.

Much can be done to improve the situation, however. Here are some concrete suggestions:

1. The Boston port should be consolidated. There are now 260 piers and wharves providing thirty miles of berthing space. This is more than we need. The surplus should be eliminated and the properties used for port-related industries, residences, and recreation. This is what the Port Authority would like to do, and what the Chamber of Commerce's Waterfront Plant proposes on a small scale.*

2. Wharves that are retained should be repaired and their equipment modernized.

3. Boston should improve rail and truck access to the port. This would make it easier for shippers to get certain commercial services and would encourage bulk loading and unloading, containerization, and other technical advances. In this way Boston

* In 1965 a plan for using part of the East Boston waterfront as a redeveloped residential area was announced.

might get a somewhat larger share of the general cargo that now goes to the congested port of New York.

4. The railroads would also do well to relinquish some of the facilities that they now operate poorly and to concentrate on modern and efficient operation of the remainder. Intown freight marshaling yards should be replaced by more compact, outlying ones. Some rail lines should be eliminated, including a few that run down city streets.

5. As we suggested in our last chapter, Boston's downtown should be zoned to help keep wholesalers' trucks from adding to the traffic congestion.

6. City and state authorities should set aside a district for a freight airport and industrial park. It should be connected by helicopter to Logan Airport.

7. The governor should see to it that the Massachusetts Turnpike Authority, the Massachusetts Port Authority, and other agencies coordinate their actions to improve freight facilities and services.

One of the points that we made about the transportation of people applies here too: It is essential to think of all transportation facilities not as separate and distinct items, but as a single, coordinated whole—a system. What Boston needs is a general strategy for the improvement of freight transportation. Such a strategy should not single out any one facility—say the port—for exclusive attention, and it should recognize that in the best system not every component can be the best possible. It is quite conceivable, for example, that the best system may leave some facilities in a less-than-ideal condition. The demand for and the technology of freight transportation are changing rapidly. New ways of moving things, new products, and new places to move them make it essential that the strategy be flexible.

Once we have the strategy, we should not render it ineffective by ill-considered public subsidies. It is a great mistake to suppose that Boston, or New England, will go to pot if this or that transportation facility is not improved. We need to improve the system as a whole, but that is not necessarily done by propping up inefficient operations at the taxpayer's expense. Doing that may only encourage further inefficiency and make matters worse both for the consumer, who in the end pays the freight, and for the taxpayer, who provides the subsidy.

There is a saying: "The wheel that squeaks gets the grease." This is the wrong principle to apply in this case. We should improve the transportation system as a whole—the parts that are not squeaking, as well as those that are—and we should do it right away.

6 Time Again for Enterprise

"We are a city too much given to croaking. I have been told that we were on the brink of ruin ever since I knew the place. Those whose duty it is to carry forward society despair of it." So said William Ellery Channing in 1836. Boston, he might have added, was founded on the very brink of ruin. The region around it was rocky, barren, and lacking in minerals. Its only advantages were its port and a moderate amount of water power on its fringes.

At the end of the Revolutionary War, the city seemed likely to slip over the brink. Britain shut off most of its trade with the West Indies and with Europe; there was nothing else to support it.

Then something happened. A few bold men responded to the challenge by opening trade routes to China and Russia and by starting a fur trade along the Columbia River.

During another war with Britain, the War of 1812, trade declined and Boston was once more on the brink of ruin.

Again something happened. This time a few enterprising businessmen founded the textile and then the shoe manufacturing industries. There was no necessity for those mills and factories to be established in Massachusetts, far from the source of raw materials. But they were established here, and Boston prospered.

To come closer to the present, it was clear even before the Depression that the textile industry was moving away and that

Note: This chapter was published in the Boston newspapers in December 1962.

12. Research-based firms sprang up rapidly on Route 128 after World War II. Here are two of the suburban parks developed by Cabot, Cabot & Forbes Company. In the foreground, on the west side of the famous circumferential expressway, is the Waltham Industrial Center. On the other side is the Waltham Research and Development Park.

Time Again for Enterprise

54

nothing could stop it. After the Second World War, its decline was very rapid: employment in Massachusetts textile plants dropped 60 percent between the end of the war and now.

Once again Boston met its crisis with a spurt of new growth. The war had set off an explosion of scientific research and technological advance in the great universities of the Boston area. Afterward, businessmen created new industries on the basis of the new knowledge. At least four hundred research-based firms came into being in the Boston region in the years following the war. The electronics industry does a business worth at least $1 billion in Greater Boston.

Military and space programs are linked to the research and electronics industries. In the fiscal year 1960, the Boston area had military contracts amounting to $630,000,000. Among the fifteen largest metropolitan areas of the country, only one — Los Angeles–Long Beach — had a significantly larger per capita share of such contracts.

It would be hard to find anything to croak about in the present situation. The future, however, is another matter. Here are some disquieting indications:

The Boston area had the smallest population increase between 1950 and 1960 of any of the fifteen largest metropolitan areas — only 7.4 percent. There are certain compensating advantages to this, but nevertheless it means that Boston's economy is not expanding.

Suburbanization is hurting downtown Boston's retail stores. These sell a third of the dollar value of goods sold in Boston. Between 1948 and 1958, their sales fell off by 4.6 percent, even though prices went up. This was less than the decline in most other large downtown districts (downtown Detroit's retail sales fell off 27.4 percent in the same period!) but the loss is serious nevertheless.

The slow population growth of the Boston area has been ac-

13. An electronics plant in a park, one of the many new facilities in the Waltham Industrial Center, west of Boston on Route 128.

companied by a shrinkage of its tributary area as population moves west. At the time of the Civil War one American in ten lived in New England. Now one in twenty lives here.

These population movements along with other factors seem to have marked New York, Chicago, and Los Angeles to be the great office centers of the nation. Only one of the 100 largest industrial firms has its headquarters in the Boston area and eight others among the 500 largest have their headquarters here.

The electronics industry has ceased to grow rapidly in the Boston area. Much new growth is taking place in Southern California, Texas, the Middle West, and in some of the small cities of Northern New England. Wages in these small cities average about 20 percent less than in Boston.

At least one job in fourteen in the Boston area is now tied to military spending. This means that a sudden end to the Cold War (an unlikely prospect, to be sure) might put us back at the brink of ruin.

What do these signs and portents mean for Boston? Perhaps some clues may be found by looking again at the record of history.

Two things stand out. One is that the events that moved Boston back from the brink were ones that could not have been predicted even a few years before. The other is that the energy, imagination, and knowledge of a relatively small number of people made those events occur.

Geography has always worked against us. But energy, imagination, and knowledge have always offset this handicap and with room to spare.

No one could have foreseen the growth of the China trade, which occurred because of the boldness of Boston merchants and sea captains. Nor could anyone have foreseen the founding of the textile and shoe industries. The inventiveness and enterprise of just a few men brought the mills and factories into being. Only a science-fiction fan could have imagined twenty years ago the vast unfolding of space, nucleonics, and other science-based industry that has taken place since.

There is no geographical or other "natural" reason why the Boston area should have become a great center of science-based industry. These industries are here because the men who founded them were here, and they were here because they liked the Boston area. In high-value, low-weight industries, a manufacturer can afford to locate where he pleases.

There was a time when the number of people involved in generating new economic activity was small. The China trade, for example, was developed by a very few.

Nowadays the generation of new activity is a complex organizational process. Enterprisers still play a crucial part in it, but they do so in close collaboration with a large staff of scientists, engineers, managers, and other specialists. New economic activity therefore tends to be located where the key personnel, as well as the enterpriser himself, choose to live.

Except as the Boston area appeals to such people it cannot sustain its present science-based industries or find new ones to take their places. Without such people, Boston would surely slip over the brink of ruin.

It is very important therefore to consider what there is about Boston that may attract or repel the gifted and highly trained people whose presence here is so essential to our prosperity.

Nothing is as important to them as the opportunity to work on exciting problems among other highly trained people. This creates a snowball effect: the more that is "going on" in an area, the greater the number of creative people who will come there; the greater the number who come there, the more there will be "going on," and so on.

In the Boston area, the great universities formed the core of a snowball which has grown very rapidly. In 1950 the area had over 13,000 engineers (to mention only one category of highly trained personnel); in 1960 it had almost 26,000 — an increase of over 90 percent. In 1960, 12.1 percent of the Greater Boston labor force did professional and technical work — a higher percentage than in New York, Chicago, Cleveland, Detroit, Pittsburgh, or St. Louis.

Next to the opportunities that it affords for exciting work, Boston will be judged as a place to live and to bring up children.

Here of course the list of considerations that may be taken into account is almost endless: the climate, the natural beauty of the countryside, the quality of schools, housing, and transportation, and the tax rate, to mention a few.

Boston gets good marks on most of these things and very high ones on some. (Even on taxes it compares favorably with other places if the comparison is with *all* taxes, not just the property tax.)

But what most distinguishes it from other metropolitan areas in the eyes of the highly trained people in question is harder to put one's finger on. It is the "feel" of Boston. This is what makes Boston really different and what attracts or repels.

This "feel" is partly myth. Boston—so some people claim—is stuffy, complacent, snobbish, backward-looking. The Bostonian, they say, went to Groton and Harvard and has led a sheltered life ever since.

The truth is that the Bostonian has contributed energetically to the economic development of the area. Not only that, he has welcomed newcomers. Of the forty-four directors of the Greater Boston Chamber of Commerce, for example, only nineteen were born in Massachusetts.

Boston is sometimes said to be corrupt—a city without civic virtue. This is also mostly myth. As compared to New York and Chicago, for example, it is probably fairly clean. There are hopeful signs, moreover, that the people of Boston intend it to become entirely clean.

(If Boston politics is not remarkably corrupt, someone will ask, how does it happen that a man in jail for larceny can be elected to the legislature? Our answer is this: the Boston political system has the defects of its virtues. In most other big cities, a boss would have kept such a man off the ticket "for the good of the party." That did not happen here because Boston has no boss. It is too bad that it happened. But it is not too bad that the city has no boss.) *

And yet the "feel" of Boston is not altogether a matter of myth. Boston has always had a special character, and it still does. It has a great symphony orchestra, great universities, a state house with a gold dome, the best medical institutions in the world, miles of old and handsome red brick dwellings in the very center of the city, no racial violence and relatively little racial hostility,†

* Perhaps because Boston is the state capital, corruption in the state government is sometimes treated as a city problem rather than a state problem. In fact the city government under Mayor Collins has been remarkably honest.

† A controversy over school segregation has increased racial feeling since this was written.

little juvenile gang warfare and teenage narcotics traffic (in some of these matters it is unique among large cities), and a political system (count this as a plus or minus as you like) that has produced leading figures in Washington.

To the gifted people upon whom its prosperity depends, these things make Boston a desirable place to live. But the historic tradition that surrounds these things is also attractive—even more so than the things themselves. The tradition is one with which many highly civilized people want to be identified.

Our main point is that the economy of Boston has prospered despite the geographic disadvantages of the region. These disadvantages have been offset by outbursts of creative energy on the part of gifted and highly trained people.

If it is to continue to prosper, the Boston area must continue to attract the most gifted businessmen, professionals, scientists, and technicians in the country. It is upon their presence that its ability to grow and to adapt to changing circumstances chiefly depends.

Particular measures to improve the economy may be less important than the forces that affect the character of the city. No doubt it would be a good thing to zone desirable sites for commerce and industry, for example. But such measures, important as they are, may be insignificant compared to others that would affect the quality of Boston as a place to live.

The recommendations we have made on the various matters we have discussed in earlier chapters—the organization of government, taxes, and transportation—are all pertinent, we think, to the question of how to strengthen the Boston economy by making Boston more attractive to highly gifted people.

In the chapters that are to come we shall discuss some other ways in which the quality of life in the Boston area can be improved and make some further suggestions for preserving and enhancing the special character of Boston.

There is no reason for croaking, then; those whose duty it is to carry forward society need not despair. If they carry it forward in the future as well as they have in the past, the commercial and industrial development of the area will flourish.

7 Which Way Downtown?

For a long time the optimists and the pessimists have been arguing about what is happening to Boston.

Boston was going to pot, they said, along with all of the other center cities in the nation. Although its downtown was choked with traffic, it was being abandoned by business. Three major stores had left downtown and one of the few national headquarters in the Boston area, that of Lever Brothers, had moved from Cambridge to Manhattan. The new scientific, manufacturing, and research firms were building on Route 128, not in the city proper, and some insurance and manufacturing firms were moving from the city to Route 128. Meanwhile, the beautiful New England countryside was being buried for miles around under a mass of highways, shopping centers, and look-alike houses.

If an optimist pointed out that Route 128 was not so very far away and that growth anywhere in the region would help Boston, the pessimist disagreed, declaring it *was* very far away, and taxes paid in the suburbs would not help to support services in Boston. If the quality of these services declined, he added, the vicious circle would tighten: more middle-income taxpayers would leave the city, the sales of the great department stores and the business of the other enterprises of the central city would fall off, it would be harder and harder to support most of the institutions that make Boston an extraordinarily good place to live and work (a good police department, museums, and the

Note: This chapter was published in the Boston newspapers in June 1964.

symphony orchestra, for example), and so still more middle-income taxpayers would leave.

The optimists point cheerfully to the many important investments that have been made in Boston in the last few years or that are planned for the next few. The most dramatic mark of confidence in the center city is the Prudential Center — a 52-story office building, a 1,000-room hotel, 75 retail shops, and two 26-story apartment buildings, all under way with private funds. This huge investment and the prospect that the city will build a convention hall have spurred private developers to renovate nearby residential and commercial properties.* Then there is the Government Center. Most of the buildings (more than $100 million worth) comprising it will be tax-exempt, but tax revenues from private development in the adjacent area will amount to more than the city collected in taxes from the whole area before construction began.

What's more, the optimists say, the Prudential Center and the Government Center are only the first swallows of the summer. More are bound to come — the remaking of the waterfront, the expansion of medical facilities, the rehabilitation of Roxbury, for example. For today's Boston, the sky is the limit.

Who is right — the optimists or the pessimists?

Our answer is: neither — and both. Boston will see more change of a kind that it will not welcome, but it is not going to pot. And more good things will follow the Prudential Center and the Government Center, but none of us will live to see Boston restored to the rank it occupied among cities in the nineteenth century.

Neither the optimists nor the pessimists seem to realize that in all metropolitan areas growth and decline occur simultaneously and that decline in one part of a metropolitan area may even be the result of growth in another.

Businesses, offices, department stores, churches, restaurants, and other activities were concentrated downtown because that part of the city was settled first. As the city grew, transportation lines were built to and from downtown, and therefore it remained the part of the city that was most accessible to all of the

* The War Memorial Auditorium to be used for conventions opened in February 1965.

other parts. Business firms that wanted to be within easy reach of the largest possible number of shoppers, employees, or clients had no choice but to locate downtown. There was also a snowball effect. Because some firms were downtown, others had to be there, too, to serve them or to be served by them.

In recent decades, downtown has ceased to be uniquely accessible, and if there is a snowball it is not a very large one. Boston's metropolitan area has grown a long way outward; thus downtown, which used to be in its center, is now on its edge. Downtown's basic trouble is that it has become relatively hard to reach from some parts of the metropolitan area.

Conceivably the metropolitan area might have grown upward in elevator-apartment houses rather than outward into low-density suburbs. But even if this had happened, it is doubtful if downtown could have continued to be as much of a hub as it once was.

Some people blame — or credit — the automobile for the movement to the suburbs. To a large extent, however, it would have taken place even if automobiles had never been invented. The mere increase in the size of the population made some spreading out necessary even if people had not wanted houses with lawns and gardens.

The huge sums that have been spent on automobiles (over 10 percent of the annual income of those who own cars) and on highways have had the effect of freeing industry and commerce from their former dependence upon railroads and mass transportation systems. This has helped to bring about the movement of industry and commerce from the central cities to the suburbs.

Now that three out of four households have cars (with 20 percent of these having a second car), many places within the metropolitan area are about as accessible to every other place within it as they are to downtown. Some, in fact, are more accessible than is downtown because one does not encounter traffic congestion in getting to them and it is easy to find a place to park when one has arrived.

Changes in business methods — the extension of assembly-line production and of new techniques for handling materials and for carrying on clerical work so as to economize on labor —

hastened the movement out of the central city. In order to employ the new methods, many businessmen required one-story buildings. This meant that they also required large tracts of inexpensive (which is to say vacant) land. Such tracts did not exist downtown.

Downtown, which used to have a monopoly on accessibility, now has competition from almost every side. Monopoly very often leads to stagnation and competition to growth and enterprise. Perhaps that is what will happen in this case. Central Boston may be led to get rid of some activities that do not really belong downtown and to strengthen others that do. Here at any rate are some of the things that we think may happen.

1. Boston will continue to grow in some directions and to retain its leadership of New England. At the same time, it will probably continue to lose certain activities to Route 128 and beyond. Those businesses or parts of businesses that are mainly billing and collecting operations, for example, are ripe for automation and some may move out of town. They are in the central city now because they once depended upon a labor force of semiskilled women clerks which could be assembled only by a public transportation system. When they no longer need this labor, they can move to the suburbs.

2. Downtown will continue to be the Boston area's main office center — the place where professional and managerial activities that require frequent face-to-face communication among decision makers are carried on. Production and record-keeping operations will be sent off to the suburbs, but top executives will remain downtown in order to be within easy reach of each other. Boston will require a great deal of new downtown office space just to replace what is obsolete. There will also be a demand for "prestige" space (the Prudential Building is an example of a prestige building). White-collar employment is increasing by about 3 percent a year nationally, and to the extent that Boston shares in this increase there will be an additional demand for new construction.

3. Boston will remain an important regional headquarters. Manhattan will generally be preferred as a location for national headquarters, and many corporations will run their New Eng-

land activities from there also; the air shuttle trip to and from Boston is no more inconvenient to the New York-based executive than the trip from his home on Long Island, or in New Jersey or Connecticut, to his office. But the convenience of travel between Manhattan and Boston may work to Boston's advantage as well. An executive who prefers the culture and way of life of the Boston area can base himself here and still be accessible to New York. Even a few new headquarters in Boston would increase the demand for downtown services very greatly.

4. Boston will hold its own as a wholesale center. The congestion in the New York wholesale districts is now so great that some of that business may be moved here or to Philadelphia in order to serve the same market area better.

5. In the interests of efficiency, some of Boston's wholesaling will doubtless move from downtown to other locations within the city that will suit them and the city better. Storage and trucking operations will probably find it advantageous to move outward from downtown, although perhaps not all the way to suburbia, but most offices and showrooms will remain where they are. This separation of wholesaling operations will occur as the firms expand their stocks and inventories to serve much larger territories. Very likely pessimists will bewail the loss of this business to downtown, but, considering how the wholesalers both contribute to congestion and are hampered by it, it is probably best for all if they are in the city but not downtown. (See Chapters 4 and 5.)

6. Downtown is best suited for retail trade in items that are unstandardized and therefore hard for the shopper to decide about—works of art, fine dresses, jewelry, cameras, rare tropical fish, and other things where a wide range of choice is desired. Such things are best sold from a central downtown location because they must draw customers from a large sales territory and because, when located near each other, they add to each other's drawing power. As incomes rise and tastes become more sophisticated, downtown sales of such items will certainly increase. Meanwhile, downtown sales of such general merchandise as is (or becomes) standardized will continue to fall.

To see why this will happen, one has only to look at recent trends. When people began moving to the suburbs, stores sprang up to sell them groceries, hardware, children's clothing, drugs and sundries. A little later a great many other things that had been sold downtown because they were expensive and hard to judge for quality (for example, furniture and household equipment) became standardized through national advertising and could then be sold in regional shopping centers. On a very minor scale, these were "downtowns" near the suburbs. Once they could get most of what they wanted at a shopping center, people went downtown much less than before. This happened not only in Boston but almost everywhere else. In 1958, sales of general merchandise were 20 percent higher outside of central business districts than inside of them in ninety-four metropolitan areas. In city after city, per capita sales inside the central business district declined. Boston's downtown has fared better than most, but it seems likely that in the future, items that are not particularly hard for the shopper to decide about—standardized ones and ones for which a wide range of choice is not desired—will be sold mostly from stores that are near where the shopper lives.

7. Downtown will continue to be a cultural and recreational center; generally speaking, concert halls, fine restaurants, nightclubs, museums, and sports arenas will not be built in the suburbs. In these matters, downtown will have competition, but most of it will be with facilities that people have in their homes. Television, hi-fi, home movie equipment, frozen gourmet dishes, and hobbies of various kinds are the competitors of the downtown concert halls, theatres, and restaurants. As the middle-income group grows in size and prosperity, it will probably turn more and more to such home-based entertainments. Like the automobile and the single-family house, TV, hi-fi, and the rest are ways of getting privacy; apparently this is something that middle-class Americans want very much. Eventually, however, the increase in home-based entertainment may lead to an increase in downtown-based entertainment, for once very sophisticated standards of taste have been formed, they can only be satisfied in theatres, restaurants, and other downtown establishments that offer a high-quality product.

8. The quality of housing will be improved to attract more people to in-town living. Luxury and near-luxury apartments will bring a good many people—especially childless couples and old people—closer to downtown. The gray areas near downtown

could be, and perhaps some day will be, put to good use. Generally speaking, the trouble with them is not that the houses are worn out or dilapidated; most of them in fact are structurally sound. Rather it is that they are too unfashionable in appearance to suit prosperous people. But tastes change, and we seem to be at the beginning of a revival of interest in Victorian architecture. Apart from this, large land-users — for example, hospitals and other institutions — will find some of these decaying gray areas well suited for their purposes.

9. The growth of the metropolitan area will continue. Tracts of single-family houses will be built farther and farther into the outskirts as population grows and incomes rise. More outlying towns will be transformed from self-contained communities into dormitory suburbs. The inconvenience of commuting will increase as settlement pushes farther out from the central city; there will be business failures in the suburbs just as there have been downtown; and the older suburbs will become unfashionable and even blighted. Meanwhile much of old Boston will have been replaced. The people who want — and can afford — something new will find it in one of two places: the very distant suburbs and the rebuilt central city. People who cannot afford high rents, a category which includes most Negroes, will find themselves increasingly welcome in the less-distant suburbs as the upper-income people turn elsewhere.

10. As long as the property tax is the main source of municipal revenue and as long as downtown provides the biggest part of the property taxes, the city government will have to give the highest possible priority to the maintenance and improvement of downtown. As we said in our chapter on "The Tax Tangle," however, Boston urgently needs a variety of additional tax sources. It is the only large city which still relies almost entirely on the property tax, and it is probably impossible to finance the kind of city-wide development that is needed from this source.

We believe that the argument that has been going on between the optimists and the pessimists is pointless. If one takes a metropolitan, rather than a purely local, point of view, there are advantages and disadvantages in almost all of the changes that are taking place.

In the long run it will be a good thing for Boston if businesses that do not belong downtown move to the outskirts of the city or to the suburbs. The places of these businesses will be taken, in all probability, by other businesses or by public activities of a kind that is peculiarly well suited to downtown locations. Perhaps we should think of an inner downtown and an outer downtown differing somewhat in their functions—the outer downtown extending as far as Boston University.

As we said in Chapter 2, there is need for metropolitan-area planning with respect to certain matters, especially transportation. As a practical matter, we said, the state government is in a better position than any other body to deal with such metropolitan problems; it should be, among other things, a metropolitan government. The new Boston Metropolitan Area Planning Council can also make a contribution to the development of a metropolitan mentality.

The time has come for the optimists and the pessimists to yield the floor to those, like the Metropolitan Area Planning Council, who think of Boston as an interrelated complex of cities and towns with a common future.

Which Way Downtown?

67

8 Housing

Housing is Boston's biggest single land use, its biggest single source of taxes, and the biggest single investment that most Bostonians make in their lifetimes.

It would cost $10 billion to replace all of the houses and apartments in the Boston region. That is more than to replace all of the factories, stores, churches, and public buildings together.

These facts do not convey the full importance of housing, however. It is the environment in which we lead our family life and bring up our children, and therefore our quality as people and the quality of our community depend upon it to a large extent.

It is disturbing, then, to learn from the Census that in Boston one dwelling in four is substandard—a higher proportion, incidentally, than in most large cities. A substandard house is not necessarily a very bad one. (To be "standard" a house or apartment must have hot and cold water, toilet and bath, no structural defects, and require no major repairs.) Nevertheless, there is no doubt that much housing both in the central city and in the suburbs is unsatisfactory.

It is mainly the consumer who decides how much and what kind of housing there is to be. If all consumers could and would pay for good housing, neither Boston nor any other city would have much of a housing problem. Private enterprise can supply good housing in the same way that it supplies automobiles, refrigerators, and ice cream cones.

Poor housing exists principally because many people's in-

Note: This chapter was published in the Boston newspapers in June 1962.

comes are too small to allow them to buy or rent good housing. Or, to put it more accurately, it exists because their incomes are too small to allow them to buy or rent good housing *as well as the many other things that they need or want* —food, medical care, cars, refrigerators, ice cream cones and all the rest.

The "housing" problem, in other words, is mainly a "too small income" problem.

But it is not simply this. Some of the people who live in substandard housing can afford good housing. They choose to live in poor housing in order to have more money to spend for other things.

In the last fifty years consumers have spent less and less of their incomes for housing. When proper adjustment is made for the change in price levels, it turns out that a consumer who would have spent say $7,500 to buy a house fifty years ago spends somewhat less for one today.*

Racial discrimination is another reason for poor housing. For example, whereas one fifth of the white families of Boston live in substandard dwellings, one half of the Negro families live in them. In part this is because the Negroes have lower incomes. In part, also, it is because they are made to pay more for good housing and to suffer inconveniences, indignities, and risks in order to get it—when they can get it at all. All this prevents them from getting as much good housing as they otherwise would.

Although the private enterprise housing market can and does supply good housing on demand, it does not work as well as it should. If it offered a spectacularly good house at a spectacularly low cost, consumers would probably spend a good deal more for housing than they do.

The housing industry has made progress. But it is still technologically backward, and, compared to other parts of our economy, its cost are still high.

There are many reasons for this. Some have to do with the nature of the house as a commodity: houses are fixed to the ground and therefore cannot be moved to places of shortage from places of surplus; they are durable and expensive and there-

---

* In the last few years consumers have reversed this trend and are spending a higher proportion of their incomes on the rental or purchase of housing.

fore not quickly replaced when they become obsolete; they are composed of many parts and much labor and therefore a change in a few parts, or even in the method of assembling some of the parts, does not affect the total cost very much.

Other reasons for the backwardness of the housing industry are to be found in the nature of the economy. Housing is the biggest single purchase that most people make. They are therefore very cautious in making it. If they think there may be a recession or depression in the offing, they postpone buying or cut down on rent. Because the consumer is cautious, the developer is cautious too. He builds only a few houses more than he has a ready market for.

Building houses is a risky business because of the sensitivity of the housing market to changes in business conditions. Its riskiness tends to prevent it from being organized on a well-financed, large-scale, industrialized basis. Even in boom times, most home builders in Boston and in other metropolitan areas build fewer than twenty houses a year.

Organized labor creates some obstacles to technological advance. The building trades have long been in the habit of trying to spread work over the year as much as possible, and this has meant resistance to the introduction of new methods and materials.

This resistance is breaking down somewhat now that building no longer depends on good weather. But the factor of labor cost in the price of a house is still disproportionately high.

Acting at the behest of some building trades unions and some manufacturers of building products, local governments in the Boston region and in most other regions have made matters worse by passing regulations to prevent the use of new materials and methods on the specious ground of public safety. Even where building codes are technically up-to-date, they generally impose needless costs on builders because of variations from town to town in what they require.

The federal government has also helped to keep the housing industry backward. Through various mortgage insurance programs, it has for thirty years made it easy for the inefficient producer of housing to get by without changing his ways.

These federal insurance programs were meant to enable the

consumer to buy housing on the installment plan. Their incidental effect has been to prevent the elimination of inefficient producers through competition.

These many impediments to the modernization of the housing industry have reinforced each other, each making the others worse. All, together, have prevented the industry from becoming organized for mass production and distribution. The housing industry does not merchandise houses in the way the automobile industry merchandises automobiles, because it is not organized on a sufficient scale. That is one reason, probably, why consumers have been spending more and more for cars.

In addition to the federal mortgage insurance programs and local codes (building codes, which regulate new construction, and housing codes, which regulate existing housing), public housing and urban renewal are the principal means by which government tries to improve the housing situation.

Both of these programs have their place, but it would be easy, we think, to overestimate how much effect they may have on the general housing situation.

Public housing (low-rent housing built and managed by government) is only a drop in the bucket. Boston has more in proportion to its total housing supply than any other large city in the North, but even so it has only 14,000 units (6 percent of all housing).

It is not at all likely that public housing will grow beyond drop-in-the-bucket size. It is accepted where low-income people must be rehoused to make way for public works projects and it is mildly approved as a way of meeting the needs of indigent old people. (Boston, which has a higher proportion of old people than any other metropolitan area, will probably get more than its share for this reason.) But the present program of public housing is not a practical or workable solution to the general housing problem because most people either are not eligible for public housing or do not like it for themselves and will not support it for others.

Urban renewal (the procedure by which a local agency buys slum properties, clears the land, and then sells it to a private developer at a reduced price, the developer agreeing to build on it in accordance with an approved plan and the federal government absorbing two thirds to three fourths of the reduction in land price as well as certain other costs) is much in the news. It causes new office buildings, civic centers, hotels, and industrial districts to spring up, and in this way it affects the destinies of the central cities profoundly. Indirectly, it has some significant consequences for housing.

Its direct effect is limited, however. What housing has been built so far anywhere in the United States as a result of urban renewal has consisted almost entirely of luxury apartments.[*]

Renewal has often inflicted hardships on the residents and small businessmen it displaced. These could have been lessened by giving more adequate compensation for direct losses. But the destruction of neighborhoods and of the close and valuable ties that people had to churches, clubs, and informal associations could not have been compensated for, and these are perhaps the worst losses of all.

The heads of the Boston Redevelopment Authority have made it clear that they will not wipe out whole neighborhoods to make way for new luxury apartments. In other cities other renewal authorities are making the same pledge.

This means that renewal — to the extent that it deals with housing — will concentrate on fixing up and repairing existing buildings and neighborhoods. It will supplement this rehabilitation work with some building here and there, but it will build large projects only in those cases where, by replacing old warehouses and other nonresidential buildings, the housing supply can be increased. Generally speaking, the cost of the new construction will be high and therefore the renewal housing will be available only to people with incomes of about $8,000 or more. Of course, making more housing available to people who are well off will, in turn, free their housing for other families whose incomes are somewhat lower.

In Boston the renewal authorities are very keenly aware of these problems. They are doing their best to avoid inflicting hardships on low-income people and to increase the supply of

---

[*] Urban renewal policies have since changed. In 1965 the Urban Renewal Administration reported that three fifths of the houses built on urban renewal land in the fiscal year 1964 were for sale or rent at prices within the reach of low-income or middle-income families.

housing for middle-income people, particularly through rehabilitating old structures.

If the picture is as we have described it, several conclusions follow:

1. The consumer is the key to the situation; if he spends more for housing, the situation will improve fundamentally; if he does not, it probably will not improve fundamentally.

2. Those people who are so poor that they cannot have good housing without depriving themselves of other essentials ought to have public assistance in adequate amounts.*

3. Up-to-date and uniform building and housing codes should be adopted and enforced for the metropolitan area — and at the same time the building trades unions should be urged to adopt a more responsible and realistic attitude toward work regulations.

4. The federal government in its housing credit programs should do what it can to make the building industry more competitive. To begin with, it should stop coddling inefficient builders.

5. Urban renewal authorities should be supported in their efforts to decrease as little as possible the supply of housing available to low-income people and to increase the supply for middle-income, rather than high-income, people.

6. We pointed out in the chapter on taxes that the local real property tax system discourages building and improvement. If the land component of real estate were taxed heavily and the building component lightly, property owners would have an incentive to put up new dwellings or to modernize old ones.

If these steps were taken, the effect would be to limber up the housing market. New firms would commit large amounts of capital for the production of housing of improved design through an advanced industrial technology. More good new housing, both for sale and rent, would be built, and therefore more good existing housing would be on the market at any one time. Middle-income families would benefit from this particularly.

If all this occurred, there might still be a housing problem:

* The national Housing and Urban Development Act of 1965 provides rent supplements for low-income people and for alternative kinds of low-rent public housing.

some people who could afford good housing might continue to live in poor housing.

We doubt, however, whether such a situation ought to be regarded as a "problem" at all. To be sure, people often make mistakes about what is good for them and they often ignore the effects of their actions on the community. But in a free society the presumption ought to lie in favor of the individual's choice, and the burden of proof ought to be upon those who say that the community should substitute its tastes and judgment for that of the individual.

Important as good housing is to Boston, some other things are as important or even more important. Freedom for the individual to live as he chooses is certainly one of them.

9 Schools

"Our common schools are a system of unsurpassable grandeur and efficiency."

Horace Mann, the founder of the Board of Education for Massachusetts, was probably not overstating the case when he wrote those words in 1845. But times have changed. In Mann's day, practically all Boston children went to the same schools. The schools were widely regarded as an indispensable means of creating a free and democratic nation.

Today the public school has declined in importance. About a third of Boston children do not attend them. In some Massachusetts cities, the proportion is even higher. In the newer suburbs, almost all children go to public schools, but these are "public" only in a very special sense since relatively few people can afford to live in such places. Like a number of other large cities, Boston is well on its way toward having what supporters of public education have always decried: segregation of children by income and therefore, to some extent, by race and religion as well.

As the importance of the Boston public schools has declined, their quality has declined too. That, at least, is what many people think. Rightly or wrongly, the general opinion is that the Boston public schools are bad.

It is impossible to say whether their present reputation is deserved. By its nature, the product of the schools — education — cannot be defined satisfactorily or measured in simple terms.

Note: This chapter was published in the Boston newspapers in February 1963.

Many Boston school buildings are old and ill-equipped, but this, of course, does not necessarily mean that the training given in them is poor. Some of the great schools of the United States are housed in buildings that are obsolete. The age and condition of buildings has much to do with safety, convenience, and attractiveness — all very important matters — but little to do with education.

By some of the other standards that are often applied, the schools look pretty good. On the average, there is one teacher in Boston for every 28.8 elementary school pupils (25 pupils per teacher is a widely accepted rule-of-thumb measure for good practice). The salary range of the Boston teacher with a bachelor's degree is $4,740 to $7,380 (in Winchester, a suburb with a reasonably good school system, the range is from $4,750 to $7,550).*

The cost of operating the elementary schools was $319 per pupil in 1961–62. (In Winchester it was $353.) Boston spends less per pupil than does New York, but about the same as some other large cities.

These figures do not tell much about the quality of the schools, however. What we really want to know is how much the pupils in the various grades are learning. This can be measured to some extent by certain nationally standardized tests. We understand that such tests have been made only in the two Latin schools.†

Benjamin C. Willis, the Chicago educator who is to conduct a study of the schools of Massachusetts, could do the people of Boston a great service by finding out how the achievement of Boston and other Massachusetts school children compares with that of children in comparable areas and by reporting the results to the public.**

Apparently there is a good deal of variation in the quality of the Boston schools. Some are much better than others.

* The legislature raised the minimum salary of public school teachers to $5,000 effective September 1, 1965. Boston and the suburbs are adjusting their salary schedules upward accordingly.

† The results of reading and arithmetic tests throughout the city schools were reported by Robert L. Levey in a feature article in the *Boston Globe* of December 14, 1964. All but one of the city's high schools were far below the national norm in both subjects.

** The Willis Commission did not take up this matter. Its recommendations, most of which were enacted into law in June 1965, called for reorganizing the State Board of Education and giving it powers to make and enforce standards.

Perhaps the reputation of the Boston school system has gone down partly because the standards by which it is judged have gone up, not because its actual performance is any worse. One can only guess about this.

In any case, the problems of the public schools are likely to get worse in the years ahead. Since 1940, enrollment in the Boston public schools has dropped by one fourth. These days more parents are sending their children to private schools. Probably many parents send their children to parochial schools not so much to give them religious training as to give them a better secular education than they think they would get in the public schools. Certainly many middle- and upper-income families have moved to the suburbs in the hope of finding better public schools.

There is little doubt that unless the reputation of the Boston public schools improves radically, this movement will continue. As average family income rises, more and more people who are seriously concerned about their children's education will be able to afford to send them to private and parochial schools or to move to the suburbs.

Probably nothing would do more to check the flight to the suburbs and preserve the character of Boston than a dramatic improvement in the reputation of its schools. Improving the schools is at least as important as urban renewal. Unless the schools are much improved, urban renewal cannot prevent the decline of the city. The mayor and other civic leaders, therefore, should put the schools high on the agenda for city improvement.

In order to bring the Boston public schools up to the high level that the situation requires, the people who run them must have greater freedom of action.

They must have freedom in their choice of teachers and they must be able to pay the high salaries necessary to attract superior personnel. They must have freedom to experiment, to innovate, and to devise courses and teaching methods that meet the special needs of particular neighborhoods and of individual pupils. They must have freedom to help the academically gifted child and the culturally deprived one.

The price of this will be high — high in money, and high in other things as well. Some established practices will have to go.

One is that of paying all teachers virtually the same amount regardless of the relative demand for the subjects they teach or the difficulty or the unpleasantness of their jobs.

The system by which teachers' salaries are set – the so-called "unified salary schedule" – is one of the main obstacles in the way of improving the schools. Under this system, which teachers' organizations insist upon almost everywhere, the differences in pay between teachers in the same school system are determined by only two factors: the number of graduate courses they have taken and the length of their service.

The result is that a kindergarten teacher may be paid more than a high school mathematics teacher – and this although mathematics teachers are in very short supply as compared to kindergarten teachers.

As matters now stand, a public school cannot offer a good mathematics teacher a high salary without offering the same high salary to all other teachers in the same category of the unified salary schedule. This means all too often that it cannot get as good mathematics teachers as it ought to have, simply because the cost of raising all teachers to the salary level that would be necessary in order to attract a good mathematics teacher would be almost astronomical.

Another practice that must go if the needs of the Boston schools are to be met is that of *rigidly* specifying the qualifications of teachers. It is essential, for example, that principals in lower-income areas be free to hire people who have the special talents required without regard to the usual certification requirements.

A teacher has every incentive to prefer to live and work in a pleasant suburb like Wellesley, where the children are easy to deal with and, in most cases, anxious to learn. To compete with a place like Wellesley for teachers, a deprived-area school must be able to offer good working conditions – convenient buildings, adequate equipment (as, for example, for remedial reading), and a stimulating atmosphere – and salaries that are considerably higher.

There is little reason to hope that the teachers' organizations will give the schools the freedom that they must have to improve themselves. There are more grade-school teachers than high-school teachers, and this is enough to assure that the unified salary schedule is not likely to be done away with. Neither is it likely that the teachers' organizations will permit relaxation of the certification requirements.

The organization of the school system needs to be drastically overhauled. The job of superintendent of schools will soon be open. This provides an opportunity that must not be missed. By bringing in a man of the highest professional attainments, the School Committee might breathe a new spirit of life into the schools. The new superintendent must come from outside Boston if that is where we can find the ablest man to provide the tough and invigorating influence that is needed.*

The School Committee should be reorganized also. About twenty years ago, the Strayer report declared that the School Committee (*not* its individual members) was not up to its tasks, and recently the Boston Finance Commission said that the division of budgetary authority between the School Committee and the mayor is unsound. If the members of the School Committee were elected for four-year, rather than two-year terms, it would probably do a better job.

We think, however, that it should be replaced by a board appointed by the mayor from among nominations made by civic organizations. This is what is done in Chicago. There the mayor appointed Sargent Shriver, now the head of the Peace Corps, as president of the Board of Education. Shriver and the other board members hired able administrators to run the schools in a highly professional way.

Such a reorganization would bring the school system closer to the mayor, whose political power a board needs to have behind it. But the schools also ought to be kept close to the public. When the more urgent organizational changes have been made, Boston should create citizens' advisory committees on a district basis. That was done in Chicago and is being done in New York.

Even if all the obstacles we have mentioned are removed, another very serious one will remain. This is the unwillingness of legislators — which is to say in the last analysis, of voters and taxpayers — to provide the much larger amounts of money that are needed to produce a first-class public school system.

* William A. Ohrenberger was appointed superintendent of schools in October 1963. He had previously been deputy superintendent.

Despite the drop in enrollment, the cost of running the schools has more than doubled since 1940. (Much but not all of this represents inflation.) If the quality of the schools is to be significantly improved, costs will rise much further in the future.

About 90 percent of what is spent for general school purposes in Boston is raised from local taxes. As we pointed out earlier, Boston cannot raise its property tax without making its long-run financial situation worse. The General Court has repeatedly refused to give the city other tax sources or to increase the amount of state aid for schools. (Incidentally, the present formula for state aid discriminates heavily against Boston and the older cities like Cambridge and Somerville.)

We seem to be in a vicious circle. The worse the reputation the schools have, the more people leave Boston for the newer suburbs. The more who leave, the less able the city is to finance improvement of the schools, and the less also its interest in doing so, for the people most concerned about schools tend to be the ones who leave.

We would like to see the Boston public schools restored to their former glory. The obstacles in the way of this are formidable, however, and we are forced to admit that the prospect of overcoming them is bleak.

If Boston cannot, or will not, give the school authorities the freedom that they must have, if it cannot, or will not, improve the organization of the school system, and if it cannot, or will not, finance the schools adequately, should it not boldly adopt, as the next best thing, a plan to encourage the growth of strong private schools?

Under such a plan, the city would make a tuition grant, with suitable public safeguards, to the parents of any Boston child who goes to a private school.* The present system penalizes parents who send their children to private or parochial schools, since they pay both taxes to support public schools and full

* This proposal provoked a flood of protest and disagreement from readers. In view of this public reaction, we have concluded that, whatever the merits of the proposal may be, it is impracticable. We would also like to point out that in offering the proposal for tuition grants we hoped (and said so) that we could "stimulate others to come up with a better, politically realistic alternative." (See last paragraph of this chapter.)

tuition at private schools. The proposal thus removes this double cost by returning to the parents a tuition allowance to be used at the school of their choice. More parents would be encouraged to make use of private schools, thus bringing into existence more and better ones, and reducing the load on, and therefore the cost of, the public school system.

The giving of such grants would greatly increase the total amount spent in Boston on education because many families would add money of their own to the grant in order to get better schooling for their children. Families of moderate means, in particular, would be able to shop around for the kind of quality in schooling that suited them—something that the well-to-do have always been able to do.

The grant system would bring into existence a large number of parochial and private schools which would compete with each other and with the public schools. These schools have a flexibility that public ones do not have. The unified salary schedule does not apply to them, and neither do the certification requirements. If one of them wants to hire a good mathematics teacher, there is nothing to stop it from paying him, or her, three times as much as the kindergarten teacher. This competition among schools should in time greatly improve the quality of Boston education.

Equally important, perhaps, the public would be more willing than it now is to be taxed for the support of schools. At present many parents who send their children to private or parochial schools feel they are getting nothing in return for their taxes. They have borne their burden with little complaint, but it cannot be doubted that they would be readier to accept new taxes if the money were to be used to educate their own, as well as other people's, children.

Some will doubtless think that the tuition grant plan amounts to a virtual repudiation of public responsibility for schooling. In our opinion, public responsibility for schools does not necessarily imply public *operation* of them. Far from intending any reduction in the responsibility of government for the education of children, we have tried to suggest a means by which, in the special circumstances that exist in Boston, that responsibility may be discharged.

Others will think that the tuition grant plan violates the principle of separation of church and state, even though the grants would be made to families and not to institutions. Even if there is no constitutional barrier to the giving of tuition grants, some may object to the plan on the grounds that it would encourage the separation of students along religious, income, class, or racial lines. It cannot be doubted that in Boston its chief impetus would be to parochial school education, and some may think this will erect barriers among religious groups.

However, we do not think that the plan would encourage any more segregation by religion, income or other groups than now exists. On the contrary, we believe that by enabling many more parents to afford private school education for their children, it would tend to break down some of the barriers which now more and more prevent the mixture of children in all the schools.

Still others may think that under the tuition grant plan the public schools would be left with none but children from very poor families and the children who come from families that place little value on education. There is no reason to believe that all the poor would be left in the public schools; presumably the tuition grant could be set high enough to pay the whole tuition of some private and parochial schools. As for the children left in the public schools, there might be some advantages in having the public school system specialized to meet their particular needs.

Finally, many may fear that the tuition grant plan might ultimately lead to political control over private schools. There is no denying that a government agency which could pass on a school's eligibility to receive students under the plan would have a power that—like all government power—might be misused. For those who think the tuition grant proposal a radical one, we should point out that for years a similar program under the G.I. Bill of Rights has enabled millions of veterans to attend recognized public, religious, or private schools of their choosing.

The tuition grant plan is one possible way of meeting the special needs of Boston. Most Massachusetts communities do not have these needs and would probably find the plan anathema.

Thus Boston faces a hard choice if it is to improve elementary and secondary school education. One choice is to restore flexibility and innovation to the public schools by radical revision of administrative controls and teaching programs, and by spending more money. We have pointed out some of the political obstacles to obtaining this objective. The tuition grant plan is hardly ideal, but it does introduce choice and competition as techniques for improving the quality of education.

Perhaps we are wrong in thinking that, failing a drastic change, deterioration is inevitable; we hope that we are. We also hope that in presenting the tuition grant proposal we can stimulate others to come up with a better, politically realistic alternative. They should do so promptly, for the hour is late.

10 Youth

To every generation of adults the youth problem appears more ferocious than it has ever been before. Reading the newspapers—juvenile delinquency, beatniks, teenage narcotics users, student riots, smash-ups, and all the rest—it is no wonder that adults begin to consider today's youth as a new breed.

Recognizing that ours is by no means the only country where youth is in a state of unrest does not help much. Britain has its "Leather Boys," Mexico its "Little Tarzans," the U.S.S.R. its "hooligans," Japan its "Chimpira," and Sweden its "Raggare." Adolescents seem to be striking out against authority everywhere.

Yet when were they not? Shakespeare certainly took a modern view of youth when he wrote in *A Winter's Tale:* "I would there were no age between 16 and 23 or that youth would sleep out the rest; for there is nothing in between but getting wenches with child, wronging the ancientry, stealing, fighting."

Until recently, "environmental conditions" were blamed when a boy or girl got in trouble. It was a broken home or a parent who drank. The underlying cause was thought to be poverty, and so it was taken for granted that as the average income rose the number of such cases would fall. Meanwhile social-work agencies would go a long way toward relieving poverty and repairing the damage that it had caused.

It is evident now that matters are not—and probably never were—that simple. Most families are well off indeed by the

Note: This chapter was published in the Boston newspapers in late May 1965.

standards of a generation or two ago. And yet our present rapidly increasing prosperity, far from eliminating juvenile delinquency, seems actually to have stimulated an increase of it.

Most of the children who come to the attention of the police live in slum or near-slum neighborhoods. In Boston, a juvenile who lives in a section of the South End is about fifteen times as likely to appear in juvenile court as one living in the Hyde Park section. But it should not be supposed that all delinquents — and still less that all deeply troubled adolescents — live on the wrong side of the tracks. In fact a good many delinquents come from the "best families" and have had every opportunity that money can provide.

Boston is remarkably typical of other cities of its size in the amount and kind of the juvenile delinquency that it has. Contrary to what may be the general impression, relatively little delinquency here or elsewhere involves violence. "Gang" rumbles have never been an important problem except in the very largest cities and even in these they are increasingly out of fashion. About two thirds of all teenage arrests are for stealing. This offense is eight times as frequent as vandalism and twelve times as frequent as assault. (Of the assaults by juveniles, incidentally, the overwhelming majority are against other juveniles, not against adults.)

In Boston, as in other cities, boys aged 15–18 are the worst offenders. Ten times as many boys as girls are arrested. When girls come to the attention of the police it is usually for running away from home, for sexual misconduct, or for refusing to accept parental discipline. Very little of the stealing by boys (or for that matter girls) involves breaking and entering. Most of it consists simply of taking something that is wanted at the moment and is easy to lay hands on.

Drug addiction is not widespread among youth in Boston, and the city's record with respect to violent youth crime compares favorably with that of other large cities. This is to the credit of the scores of agencies in the city that deal directly with children — the police, probation officers, courts, social workers, settlement houses, city recreation department, athletic associations, guidance clinics, boys' clubs, and, of course, the schools and churches. The Youth Activities Board, an agency in which

Mayor Collins has shown particular interest, has helped prevent the growth of violent juvenile gangs. The Boston Police Department shows great patience and tact in its handling of juveniles, and the Federal Bureau of Narcotics is doing a magnificent job of ferreting out addicts and "pushers."

The majority of the juvenile delinquents are petty offenders who will not become hardened criminals. A few of them — very few, fortunately — suffer from some form of mental illness. Most, however, are in good mental health.

This is true also of the large number (no one can say how large) of adolescents who, although not delinquent, are nevertheless profoundly at odds with the world. Especially among boys and girls who come from the "right" side of the tracks, youthful restlessness and rebelliousness are likely to take forms that are nonviolent but nevertheless self-destructive. Hating or fearing "the system," or being bored by everything, may lead to action (or inaction) that is harmful not only to the boys and girls themselves but to others as well.

The great majority of adolescents, even among those in trouble, are essentially normal. But normal adolescence, it must be added, is a very confused and confusing state. A normal boy or girl between the ages of about fifteen and twenty-three may be in a condition of inner turmoil that even a very sympathetic adult finds hard to comprehend.

The adolescent himself does not know what is troubling him, and he is apt to suppose that, whatever it is, it will go on forever. According to psychologists, however, his preoccupations center around a few themes, and these are likely to be much the same regardless of income, race, or background.

The adolescent is preoccupied above all, the psychologists say, with questions about his identity. He keeps wondering who he is, what he is, and where he is headed. He wonders how his abilities compare with other people's and what others think of him. If he is a boy, he is likely to be particularly concerned about his masculinity. He is afraid he is not as much of a man as he should be, and he looks for opportunities to prove to himself and to others that this is not the case.

As it seems to the adolescent (and he is largely right about this), the only way to find out what one is really like is to try first one thing and then another. He or she is therefore engaged in a ceaseless effort to test himself, to see if the world is the way it seems to be, to find out what will happen if . . .

This is a kind of brinkmanship, and like all brinkmanship it is dangerous. There is no way that it can be made safe, for once it is safe it ceases to serve its purposes, which is to see how far one can go before . . .

At the same time that he is discovering who and what he is, the adolescent is moving from the dependent position of a child to the responsible one of an adult. Insofar as he is a child, he must do what he is told and he need take no responsibility. But insofar as he is an adult, he must take responsibility for the welfare of others. Moving from one condition all the way to the other in the short space of five or six years requires learning a great deal. In the most confusing period of his or her life, the young person must somehow learn how to be an adult.

Coming to terms with reality is a part of this process. In early adolescence a boy or girl finds it almost impossible to distinguish fantasy (what it would be nice to have happen) from fact (what is actually possible or likely). Many mistakes are made because in the early morning of life the rough places are hidden behind thick clouds of fantasy.

The adolescent is also a healthy young animal, of course. He or she often has a need for almost incessant physical activity, for thrills and excitement (often involving an element of physical danger), and for "having fun." It goes without saying that at a certain age "having fun" involves the opposite sex and may become an intense and even painful preoccupation.

Much of the behavior that we all deplore is a manifestation of the normal, and more or less necessary, confusion that occurs in the process of growing up. Stealing, for example, may seem to a boy to be a good way of proving to himself and his fellows that he is smart, bold, and willing to take risks. It is also, of course, a way of generating excitement. Similarly, sex and liquor parties, marijuana smoking, and—in a few cases—violent crimes are means by which some boys try to reassure themselves about their masculinity or, as they would probably put it, prove that they are not "chicken." Dangerous driving—hot-rodding or otherwise—property destruction, unruly gatherings like the recent one at Hampton Beach—are all, we suspect, expressions of the adolescent's desire to get excitement through risk.

If it is normal for adolescents to act most of the time as if they were sleepwalkers on a high wire, it is also normal for them to wake up eventually and, perhaps, to shudder at the risks they ran. Most troubled boys and girls, and most juvenile delinquents as well, turn out to be respectable—sometimes even stodgy—citizens in the end.

After a boy marries and has children he usually ceases to worry about being masculine and finding excitement. He no longer has to prove anything to himself or to others and, besides, "getting into trouble" is a much more serious matter than before. If he gets into trouble he may lose his job. And then what will his wife say? And how could he face his children?

The community's problem, therefore, is to deal with normal people in a rather brief but very trying period of their lives. Once they are past adolescence all will be well in most cases.

Much can be done to reduce juvenile delinquency by eliminating some of the temptations and opportunities that are now open to the juvenile. The installation of vandal-proof parking meters, for example, will prevent a good many boys from getting in trouble. If motorists would take the trouble to lock their cars, that would help too. Joy-riding in stolen cars is a major problem in Boston, as it is in most other large cities.

There is good reason to believe that preventive measures of these sorts (improved street lighting is another example) reduce the *total* amount of delinquency, not just cause a shift from one kind of delinquency to another. Stealing is, as we said, by far the most frequent offense, and it does not take much to deter the juvenile would-be thief.

On the other hand, there is no doubt that the adolescent's restless desire to test himself, to find out by trial and error what the world is like, and to have thrills must and will be expressed in one way or another. Perhaps it is because urban life is so "tame" that youth seeks the kinds of excitement that it does. Boys cannot even shoot off firecrackers on the Fourth of July; community fireworks are the rule. Halloween has been turned from a time of pranks to the collection of candy, or even pennies for UNICEF. Universities, which traditionally provided a controlled avenue for the periodic expression of aggression, have grown larger, more purposeful, and more sensitive to public opinion. Nowadays one seldom hears the phrase "boys will be boys."

Some social scientists think that the success of the big cities in curbing violent youth gangs has had the indirect effect of causing adolescents to take up marijuana and even heroin instead. The gang fighting created some serious injuries, but the gang members in most cases grew up eventually and put their leather jackets aside. Addictive drugs, on the other hand, not only destroy the individual who uses them but may cause him to inflict injuries on others.

In view of these considerations, we think that the strategy of the community ought to be to try to channel the energies of youth into wholesome outlets to the greatest extent possible and, failing this (for there will always be a good many boys and girls who will feel compelled to do things that are wrong and self-destructive), to channel them to the kinds of antisocial behavior which are least likely to do permanent injury to the young people themselves and to others.

If changes could also be made in the handling of youthful offenders, then antisocial boys and girls might not be let off too leniently nor be pushed into becoming more antisocial. For example, if punishments more severe than probation but less severe than reform school were developed—weekend detention is a possibility—it would be easier to make young people take thought for the consequences of their illegal activity.

It is one thing to talk about finding wholesome outlets for youthful energies and another thing to find them. Those adolescents who constitute the most serious part of the problem are not going to be satisfied with sand-lot baseball games and the kinds of organized recreation that a settlement house or a city department can provide. They want (among other things) the taste of danger—the danger of losing life or limb, not of losing a game—and there is obviously no safe way of giving them that. Drag-racing (on a specially designed course to protect the non-racers) is one form of recreation that has the appeal of danger.

This has been tried in several communities and might be tried in Boston.

But a generation or two ago a boy tested himself the hard way by going to work at a tough and perhaps risky job. At the age of sixteen or seventeen he went to work as a man among men. The work gave him the physical exercise that he needed, and it gave him also an opportunity to test his qualities—ingenuity, endurance, courage, and the rest—against those of others. He got the reassurance about himself that he needed, he learned to accept responsibility, and he found a certain measure of excitement (sometimes a great deal of it) all as incidental features of the job. The job was a means of making a living, of course, not a course of occupational therapy, but it served some basic psychological needs all the same.

Today we make it hard for a boy to accept the discipline of a tough job. No matter how strong he may be physically and how unwilling he may be to learn from books, we keep him in school, usually under the direction of women teachers, at least until he is sixteen. Then we label him "drop-out," which is equivalent to "failure," if he leaves without graduating. Once he is out of school, we treat him as unemployable and if he remains unemployed we ignore him.

This is exactly the wrong way to channel the energies of youth, in our opinion. We believe that there are many boys and girls (from prosperous as well as poor families) who have learned as much in school as they can, or at any rate will, by the age of fifteen. They should be encouraged to leave school—perhaps a good many of them will return to it when they are older—and go to work. Those of them who have the ability and inclination to do so may acquire skills on the job as apprentices; many, however, will remain unskilled.

To enable boys and girls to leave school when they have stopped learning without being labeled "drop-outs," graduation should be at the end of the tenth year of school. The present high school education falls between two stools: it is more than is needed by those who are to be unskilled workers and not enough for those who are to be skilled. We are not, we hasten to add, in favor of letting anyone drop out of school for lack of money; a boy or girl with the interest and aptitude to gain by continuing to go to school or college should certainly be assisted to do so.

Those who do graduate from school in the tenth grade should have opportunities to get more formal training in night schools, through supervised reading at public libraries, and in other ways that might be devised. Those who decide after a year or two of working that they made a mistake in not going on to college should be enabled to remedy the mistake.

President John Hannah of Michigan State University recently objected to the idea "that everyone should have at least 12 years of schooling and that when anyone drops out of school before he graduates from high school, it is the fault of our educational system." Then he added, "If we want our schools to be custodial institutions for all individuals up to the age of 18 or so, that is one thing. If we want them to be agencies of education, that is something else. Schools deserve to be told which it is to be. And the decision is one to be made by all of our people, not by educators alone."

The recommendation made recently by the Massachusetts Education Committee that the school-leaving age be raised to eighteen is unwise, in our opinion. Forcing an unwilling youth to remain in school not only deprives him of the discipline of a job and undermines his self-respect but impedes learning by other pupils. In this way it destroys the morale of both the pupils and the teachers.

Not every job will provide sufficient scope and challenge for the energies of a vigorous boy. The right kind of job will be in an environment of men, especially of men who do work in which there is an element of risk. Construction workers, telephone linemen, truck drivers, firemen, and policemen are examples.

It will be objected that there are not enough jobs of any kind to go around, let alone jobs of this particular type for untrained boys. The situation could be changed. If minimum-wage laws and union rules were revised so as to permit and encourage the employment of youthful helpers, trainees, and apprentices, many jobs of the kind that are needed could be opened. (New York City has begun hiring eighteen-year-olds as apprentice policemen; this is a step in the right direction.)

The number of suitable jobs could be expanded further by paying a subsidy to private employers who will take adolescents as trainees. This is being done on an experimental scale

14. A broken window is repaired in Roxbury by trainees in the work-crew project of the youth training and employment program conducted by Action for Boston Community Development (ABCD).

by Action for Boston Community Development (ABCD), a non-profit corporation established in 1961 by a group of Boston leaders and financed by the Ford Foundation, several local foundations, and the federal government. ABCD's experience along these lines may be given wider application eventually by the newly created Youth Opportunities Center of the Massachusetts Employment Service.

To the extent that jobs of the normal sort cannot be found for adolescents who want and need them, provision should be made through public facilities. The camps which the newly organized Youth Corps is establishing in Massachusetts and elsewhere are an example of the sort of thing that we have in mind. Boston City Councilor William J. Foley, Jr. has suggested that the federal antipoverty program be used to get youth in the battle against slums. Ideally two objectives would be well served: the constructive employment of young people and the rehabilitation of property, the repair of which would be too costly under conventional methods. Suggestions such as these deserve the most careful consideration.

We are not under the delusion that we have suggested any general solution to the problems of juvenile delinquency and unrest. Indeed, the thing we feel surest about is that there never can be any such solution.

Channeling the energies of youth into more constructive (or less destructive) outlets—especially work—would help. So would removing the removable temptations. So would relieving boys and girls who cannot or will not learn in school of the boredom and humiliation of wasting time there. So would changing the legal system of dealing with youthful offenders.

But we should recognize that powerful forces are working to put ever more difficult demands upon youth. As the general level of wealth and skill in our society rises, the adolescent has more and more to learn. Perhaps the best thing that the adult can do is to let adolescents know that they do not all have to fall into the same time-table or the same pattern.

Youth

11 Law and Order

One of the marks of a good community is a low rate of major crime. By this standard, Boston's record is remarkable even when one takes into account the many stranglings that have occurred in recent years.

Of the twenty-one metropolitan areas with populations of over one million, only seven (Buffalo, Cincinnati, Cleveland, Milwaukee, Paterson, N.J., Pittsburgh, and Philadelphia) had fewer major crimes per 100,000 population than did Boston in 1961.*

Some metropolitan areas had crime rates twice as high as Boston's. Compared to the average of about two hundred metropolitan areas, Boston's record is strikingly good for every kind of major crime except auto theft. Here are the latest F.B.I. figures on crimes per 100,000 population.

	Boston metropolitan area	Average of all metropolitan areas
Murder	2.3	4.6
Rape	4.5	10.5
Robbery	34.5	74.2
Assault	35.4	93.8
Burglary	443.9	630.9
Larceny	277.6	405.3
Auto theft	464.3	281.9

Note: This chapter was published in the Boston newspapers in late April 1963.

* Still true in 1963, the latest year for which F.B.I. figures are available as this book is made ready for publication in 1965. In the table on this page, we have substituted the F.B.I.'s 1963 figures for the 1961 figures that appeared in our original article. However, in 1964 and 1965, Greater Boston hoodlums committed at least 28 murders and a dozen attempts at murder.

Compared to the narcotics problem that exists in New York, Chicago, and some other large cities, Boston's narcotics problem is small.

There is also relatively little juvenile delinquency here. In the average American city, more than 14 percent of the persons arrested are children aged 16 or less; in Boston, fewer than 8 percent are so young. In most cities, the number of juvenile arrests has been increasing in the last few years; in Boston it has been decreasing. Teenage gang fights and "rumbles" are a very serious problem in New York. Boston has some gangs, but nowhere near as many (even taking account of the difference in size between the two cities) as New York.

The F.B.I. does not publish comparative figures on arrests for vice, disturbances of the peace, and traffic violations, but there seems to be no reason to believe that Boston is any worse in these respects than other large cities.

Strange as it may seem, one factor in explaining Boston's relatively low crime rate is probably the weather. Almost everywhere, people commit more crimes of certain types—especially crimes against persons as distinguished from property—when the weather is hot. Boston has fewer crimes in winter than in summer ("Snow and cold weather," a senior police officer told us, "are our best policemen") and Northern cities have fewer than Southern ones. The crime rate is low throughout New England. It is lower in Boston, however, than in such other cool cities as Chicago, Detroit, and Seattle.

Another factor that influences a city's crime rate is the nationality, racial, and class composition of its population. Both the amount and the kind of crime that occurs in a city depend to some extent upon the cultural background of the people. Here also Boston seems to have a long-standing advantage.

A third factor is the effectiveness of the police and the courts in enforcing the law. That the crime rate is relatively low here strongly suggests that the Boston law enforcement agencies are doing at least a reasonably good job.

We do not have a good explanation to offer on Boston's bad record on auto thefts. The rate is high (although not as high as in Boston) throughout New England. Most stolen cars are not resold; they are used for joy rides and then abandoned. Perhaps one explanation is that a relatively large number of automobiles are parked on the streets here.

That the various murders are as yet unsolved, and are therefore very much in our minds, should not distract attention from the fact that the record of the Boston police (we refer here to the police of the city proper, not of the metropolitan area) in solving major crimes is at least as good as that of the police in the average large American city. Here are the figures for 1963: *

Percentage of offenses
cleared by arrest

	Boston	Average of 49 largest cities
Murder	83	91
Rape	91	68
Robbery	38	39
Assault	84	75
Burglary	26	27
Larceny	44	20
Auto theft	21	23

This is not to say that the Boston taxpayer is getting as much for his money as he should. Boston spends more per capita on its police force than any other large city — $26.40 in 1960 as against $17.26 for the average city of over half a million population. Even New York, which has a very difficult police problem, spent only $22.28.

Boston has a great many policemen — 4.0 per thousand population in 1961 as compared to 1.9 per thousand for the average large city. It is the number of policemen, not their rate of pay, that makes the total cost so high. One reason why the city has so many policemen is that its daytime population is more than doubled by many thousands of commuters, shoppers, and students who create traffic problems and require protection. Another is that the police drive ambulances, guard school crossings, patrol the harbor, take the census, and do numerous other things not generally done by policemen in other cities.

These "extra" functions, not performed by the police depart-

* In our article as originally published, the figures for 1960 were used.

ments of most large cities, require the services of about four hundred men and cost at least $3,000,000 a year. Since they have to be performed by someone, there would not necessarily be any advantages in transferring them from the police department, but it should be remembered that the presence of these "extras" in the budget makes the cost of police services appear larger than it really is.

But even if one takes into account that the Boston police do more things than most police departments do, it seems fair to say that the taxpayer is not getting as much for his money as he should.

Considering its low crime rate and large police force, one might expect the Boston department to be the best in the country. It is probably pretty good—better at any rate than many Bostonians give it credit for being—and now that the commissioner is appointed by the mayor rather than the governor it is probably getting better. But it is certainly not the best in the country. What can be done to make it so?

Experts on police administration agree that the crux of the problem of organization is to make the best possible use of police officers' time. It is easy to see why. About 90 percent of a large police department's budget is for personnel. This is why the recent Tamm Survey * of the Boston police department stresses ways to get more for the dollar spent on wages.

We suggest four main directions for improvement:

1. *Improve the policeman's morale.* In every occupation, people work best when they think that their work and the organization for which they do it are both worthy of respect and respected. In the nature of things, the policeman and the public cannot be on easy terms with each other: it is unavoidable that each must regard the other with some suspicion. That policemen as such are not generally liked is enough in itself to create a morale problem. (What does a policeman say when his children ask him why it is that on TV "private eyes" are alert and smart while "cops" are dumb?)

* An outside consulting study directed by Quinn Tamm, executive director of the International Chiefs of Police, Incorporated, of Washington, D.C.

Anything that indicates public respect for law and for the policeman as an agent of law enforcement will tend to heighten the policeman's self-respect and to improve his morale. There is, of course, no substitute for real respect. But to the extent that this exists, certain outward marks — handsome uniforms, for example — make it visible and help to reinforce it.

We think the police mounts used to control pedestrian traffic downtown would be worth all the hay and grain they eat if they served no purpose but to make the police force a little more glamorous in the eyes of the ordinary citizen. Glamor doesn't necessarily engender respect, but it helps. We would like to see the Boston policeman as much respected as the Canadian Mountie or the London Bobby.

The most obvious and indispensable way of indicating public respect for the policeman would be to pay him more. Recently Governor Peabody signed legislation permitting cities to pay policemen a minimum salary of $6,300 after three years service. The present minimum is $4,880 and the maximum $5,500. The Tamm Survey recommended an increase and so has Mayor Collins. It seems plain to us that the objective — a smaller but better police force — cannot be attained in any other way.

A pay increase, Commissioner McNamara says, would both increase morale and help to attract a higher calibre of recruit. The city will get more for its money, he says, by raising pay than by increasing the size of the force.*

Incidentally, few people realize that policemen are required to appear in court on their own time. If the policeman is on a daytime tour of duty, court attendance is counted as duty. But if, as is more likely, he is on one of the two night watches, he must appear on his own time with no compensation other than the token witness fee of $3 a day. An officer who has had a strenuous night's duty may have to go to court after having had only three or four hours' sleep and then the case may be continued until the next day, which means that he will lose his sleep again. We believe that officers should be paid for all of the time they spend on duty.

Another way to improve morale is to weed out incompetent or dishonest officers. There are not many of these, but the few

* The policemen's pay was raised by $1,000 by a referendum vote in 1964.

15. Police Station 11 on the job. "We would like to see the Boston policeman as much respected as the Canadian Mountie or the London Bobby."

there are weaken the confidence of the public not only in the police force but in all government and in the very idea of rule by law. The public's loss of confidence then tends to lower the morale of the police. From the standpoint of the public and of the good police officer, it would be better to give the policeman less job security and more money instead.

2. *Give the policeman better training.* The public would get more for its money by improving the training of policemen than by using the same amount of money to employ more of them. Think of the time — not only his own but other people's as well — that is wasted by a policeman who does not know how to gather and present evidence so that it will be accepted in a court. The errors that a policeman makes are almost always costly.

The Boston police department is aware of this need and is trying to meet it. Its facilities are not adequate, however. We believe that Massachusetts should operate an academy at which rookies from all police departments in the state could receive a six-month training course.* In addition, specialists should be sent to the F.B.I. and other police schools for training in highly technical work.

3. *Free the policeman from non-police duties.* The Tamm Survey recommends that the police not be used to take the census or guard school crossings. In general it certainly makes sense not to use policemen for work that could as well be done by others whose time is less valuable. Where the service is one that would have to be performed anyway and might cost more if it were performed outside the police department—ambulance service is a case in point—the argument for separating it from the police department is not so strong.

Better use of mechanical aids is one means by which the policeman's time could be made to go further. Take, for example, a very simple matter: the marking of streets in the central business district. Having been laid out in the first place by cows that were wandering to and from their pastures, the Boston streets are the worst maze to be found in any American city. People are forever making wrong turns and getting lost. Straightening them out and getting the traffic that they have impeded back into motion takes a lot of the policeman's time. If the streets were clearly marked, traffic would move faster and fewer policemen would be needed.

4. *Make the policeman more mobile.* At present Boston has fifteen district headquarters plus one harbor division, each with its own patrolmen, detectives, juvenile officers, clerks, and lock-up. In effect, these practically constitute fifteen police departments. The Tamm Survey recommends elimination of many of the district headquarters, assignment of personnel from the central headquarters to whatever part of the city they are needed in on a particular day or even a particular hour, and the use of

* In 1964 the legislature established a Municipal Police Training Council and required that all rookie policemen in cities and towns of more than 5,000 population attend a training school approved by the council.

one-man patrol cars in place of foot patrol. In general, the idea is to move policemen around so as to use their time to better advantage. Some of the recommendations have already been put in effect. One station has been closed and a tactical squad created.

There is, to be sure, something to be said on the other side of these questions. Some think that under the present decentralized system the officers get to know their districts intimately and are therefore better able to prevent crimes from being committed and to put their finger on persons suspected of having committed crimes. A good many matters that would go to court under a centralized system may be settled informally on the curbstone by a policeman who knows his district well. These are all important considerations. Some of them, however, cut two ways (perhaps many matters that are settled on the curbstone *ought* to be brought into court), and our guess is that the Boston department could be centralized a great deal without much sacrifice of these values.

The general object towards which all four of these suggestions point and towards which the Police Department itself seems to be energetically striving is a police force consisting of fewer men but of men who are better qualified, better trained, and, of course, better paid. Such a force would not cost the taxpayers any less than the present one, in all probability, but it would give them more for their money.

Law enforcement is not just a matter of protecting the innocent and catching the criminal, of course. Unless the courts operate effectively to punish the guilty and to instill respect for law—including, it should be emphasized, respect on the part of the police for the rights of citizens whether they be law offenders or not—no police department, however well-organized and efficient, can perform its task well. In the larger task, therefore, which is the maintenance of law and order and the dispensing of justice, the police, the bench, and the bar must all work as one. Boston deserves a model police force, but it can have one only as part of a model system for the just enforcement of law.

12 Beauty in the City

Among the grounds for awarding Boston the title of "All-America City," emphasis was given to the large number of important new buildings that are planned or underway. Strangely, nothing was said about the *quality* of these new buildings or, more generally, about Boston's recent achievements in making itself a more beautiful city.

The appalling ugliness of most American cities has long been a subject for comment abroad and embarrassed silence at home. Some of our large cities are either magnificent or charming. Manhattan, Washington, Chicago, and San Francisco are — each in its way — grand and moving. Philadelphia and New Orleans are intimate, human, and delightful. Boston — need we say? — has some of the best of both of these worlds: it is magnificent *and* charming, grand *and* delightful.

It is true, however, that most American cities are ugly, and that even the cities we have named are beautiful only in certain places and from certain perspectives. Louisburg Square is as delightful as a London residential square; Commonwealth Avenue is one of the world's great boulevards; the Fenway, laid out by Olmsted, is unexcelled anywhere; Bulfinch's State House, his handsome houses on Beacon Hill, and his building at the Massachusetts General Hospital, H. H. Richardson's Trinity Church, and McKim, Mead and White's Boston Public Library are all achievements of which any great city might be proud.

Note: This chapter was published in the Boston newspapers in late June and early July 1963.

16. Louisburg Square "is as delightful as a London residential square."

It is not just the excellence of separate structures that makes a great city beautiful, of course, and Boston has the other things that are required—the appropriateness of buildings one with another, open space, scale, a highway network that contributes to civic design.

Having said this, we must add, however, that there are parts of the city that are altogether lacking in grandeur or charm, and that some of it is a shambles and a dirty one at that.

There are, we think, three main reasons why the average American city is so lacking in beauty as compared to the European one. The first is that throughout our city-building period we

17. Commonwealth Avenue, one of the world's great boulevards, as seen from above, cutting a wide trench down the center of the picture. Another kind of thoroughfare, the Massachusetts Turnpike Extension, is at lower right. Camera points eastward. Photo in October 1965.

18. Bulfinch's State House, surmounting Beacon Hill and facing Boston Common. The gold-domed seat of Massachusetts' government (architect, Charles Bulfinch) is shown from an unusual angle.

have been richer than the Europeans. The second is that among us there has been vastly more respect for the right of the individual to have, do, and be what he pleases. The third is that our cities have been governed more democratically in the sense that popularly elected local officials have had more to say about the conduct of local affairs.

It may seem odd to argue that wealth, respect for the tastes of individuals, and democracy have made our cities ugly, but the evidence is not hard to find. The beautiful cities of the Old World were in most cases laid out by monarchs, nobles, and prelates who had absolute power and who cared not a whit for the convenience or welfare of ordinary people. (The great boulevards of Paris, for example, were created partly so that the authorities might use cannon against street mobs.)

Today the cities of Europe are only beginning to enjoy the opportunities to create ugliness that we have had. Belgrade, a Communist official proudly said not long ago, will soon have automobiles enough to be congested in the American manner. Recently London saw the opening of the first building tall enough to invade the privacy of the gardens of Buckingham Palace. Now that European cities have become more prosperous and more aware of public opinion, they are turning avidly to the production of what we in this country have long been derided for, "urban sprawl." Poverty itself, of course, was never a guarantee of civic beauty (the industrial cities of Lancashire and the Saar are proof of that), but prosperity certainly opens new opportunities for bad taste.

Boston's special position as one of the few beautiful cities of America is to be explained on the following grounds.

Since it is one of the oldest cities in the country, much of it was built in a pre-industrial period; therefore, it has a great many structures with the simplicity and charm of an age which could afford nothing worse. Having been laid out long before the automobile was dreamed of and having a hilly and irregular topography, it had character, variety, and interest as well as a natural resistance to sprawl.

For a long time, too, Boston was governed by an aristocracy of wealth and taste. A long line of rich, cultivated, and public-spirited businessmen ran the city in a manner that was both high-handed and liberal. Men like Charles Francis Adams, for example, insisted upon establishing a system of metropolitan parks and forest preserves. Others brought the Boston Public Library and other such great civic enterprises into being without much consultation with the voter or the man on the street.

After the first World War, the city beautification movement lost its impetus not only in Boston but elsewhere as well. The reason was, perhaps, that the old aristocracy had lost much of its political power and its younger representatives had come to believe that measures to relieve poverty and social injustice should take precedence over projects for city beautification.

19. Richardson's Trinity Church, completed in 1877 (architect H. H. Richardson), is on the east side of Copley Square.

20. Boston Public Library, on the west side of Copley Square, facing Trinity Church, was designed by McKim, Mead & White and completed in 1895.

In the last fifteen years we have reached new heights of prosperity and local democracy, but in this time we have destroyed a not insignificant part of that which we inherited from the past. It is because we are rich and because we want to use our wealth to give ordinary people opportunities for better living that we are destroying some of the fine buildings and streets of the past in order to make way for expressways and renewal projects. If it were indifferent to the plight of the slum dweller, Boston would not have so many painful choices to make.

It is because American cities today are very democratically governed that they are not putting up many great buildings. Recently a jury of the City Club of New York, after examining twenty-four municipal structures, including schools, public housing projects, court buildings, piers, and hospitals, decided by a three-to-one vote not to award any citation for excellence in civic architecture. Nothing worthy of an award had been built by a public body since 1958, the jury said.

As everyone knows, many excellent buildings have been built in New York in this period by private enterprise. Why is it that private enterprise creates beautiful structures when public enterprise does not? One would think it would be the other way around since a private enterprise (those of them that are run for profit at any rate) has no way of charging the consumer for the satisfaction he gets from the sight of the building and therefore no business incentive to spend more than necessary on the design of the building. A public body, on the other hand, exists for the purpose of serving the public and may expect its reward at the polls.

There are several reasons for this anomalous state of affairs. Some businessmen think that putting up a beautiful and famous building will contribute to the prestige of their companies and ultimately to profits. Others think that the company has an obligation to serve the community in this way even at some cost to the stockholders. But whatever the businessman's motives, once a building has been decided upon he has a relatively free hand in the choice of design.

The public official is in a very different position. He knows that somebody will criticize him if he "wastes" even a few dollars on the beauty of a building. He knows, too, that an architecturally excellent building is very likely to be controversial. No one will criticize him if he plays it safe with a conventional building.

Boston, along with other American cities, is now entering a new era of development—one in which still greater wealth and democracy will lead to civic beauty rather than civic ugliness. Whereas this generation has been prosperous enough to build millions of comfortable homes and to expand public services in all directions, it has not been prosperous enough to build millions of homes that were beautiful as well as comfortable or to house its expanded public services in magnificent public buildings. Barring some great catastrophe, the next generation will be rich enough not only to build but to build beautifully.

In the last fifteen years the median family income in Boston doubled, and it may double again in the next fifteen years. Bostonians can afford more civic beauty just as they afford more schooling, more cars, and more steaks.

As the average income of the community increases, a larger proportion of the people learn to enjoy and to want the satisfactions that come from art in all its forms. There was a time not so long ago when art was the possession of the few. Democracy tended then to be hostile toward it because it was alien and seemed to reflect somehow on democracy itself. Now that the business of providing for material needs is not so urgent or all-absorbing, large numbers of people are seeking for the first time to enjoy sophisticated works of art. That thousands and thousands of people would stand patiently in line for an eight-second view of the Mona Lisa is indicative of this growing popular taste. So is the "success" of the Metropolitan Museum of Art in spending $2,300,000 for a single painting. How genuine or significant the aesthetic experience of the hundreds of thousands who went to see these paintings is a question, of course, but one that is aside from our present point, which is that millions of people are trying as best they can to enjoy what they have learned to think is beautiful.

It would be a great mistake to suppose, merely because they do not stand in line and pass through a turnstile, that great numbers of people do not also want to see great architecture and

21. Boston's new city hall, west perspective, architect's drawing. The building is under construction in the new Government Center as this book goes to press.

great civic design. It may well be that more people will get more pleasure from looking at Boston's new city hall than from looking at Rembrandt's painting of Aristotle Contemplating the Bust of Homer.

Assuming that we are right in thinking that the people want to enhance the beauty of the city, the city government has a clear responsibility. For the reasons that we mentioned, private profit-making enterprises cannot be expected to spend as much on good design as the public would like to have spent. Because the benefits of it go to everyone and therefore cannot be charged for on a fee-for-service basis, civic beauty, like national defense, must be the concern of the public authorities. Even the hardest-bitten advocate of free enterprise cannot object to public provision of goods which, like these, cannot be provided in the amounts that people want through the operation of profit-seeking.

Certainly, all public buildings, even the most routine and out-of-the-way, ought to be regarded as opportunities for great architectural achievement. This means that the city must seek

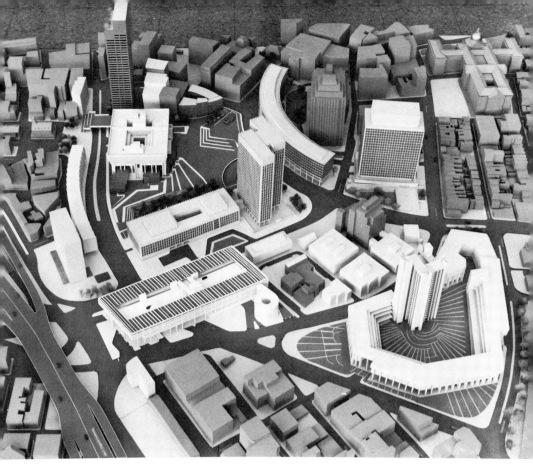

22. Model of the Government Center, prepared by the Boston Redevelopment Authority. View is approximately southward. The Central Artery (elevated highway) is at lower left. Buildings shown in white are new or under construction. By early 1966 the Federal Office Building (2 and 3) and the State Office Building (6) were already up. The old County Courthouse (5) and State House (7) are included in the small sketch to show their locations in relation to the new structures.

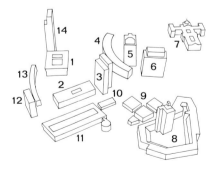

1. City Hall
2 and 3. Federal Office Building
4. Private office building
5. Suffolk County Courthouse
6. State Office Building
7. State House
8. State service center
9. Private office buildings
10. Police station
11. Parking garage
12 and 13. Motel-office complex
14. Private office tower

out great (but not necessarily famous) architects and give them the freedom, not only in essentials but in details as well, without which great art is impossible.

Boston has shown in the case of the new city hall that it knows how to proceed. The design of that building was chosen from an open competition in which there were 256 entries. Many other cities have had similar competitions, but few indeed have given the job to the winner. Boston did give the job to the winner, and, as Eric Larrabee has written in *Horizon* (January 1963), "This near-miracle can be attributed in part to the courage of Mayor John F. Collins, in part to the energetic Government Center Commission, and in part to the leading architects of Boston . . ."

We also believe that the city should take steps to help make private structures more beautiful. We recommend that the city, to secure for the public the benefits of better design, require that the builder of any structure employ a registered architect. The requirement that registered architects be used is no more un-toward than the requirement that practice before a court of law be restricted to members of the bar. In the case of both profes-sions such a regulation can provide only for competence, not for greatness.

At the very least, the city must avoid steps which would dis-courage private parties from beautification efforts. New York City recently raised taxes on the Seagram Building by one third of a million dollars a year on the ground that by building so beautiful a building the company had enhanced its prestige and value. If this decision stands (the company is appealing it), other companies will probably take steps to avoid any suspicion of architectural excellence for fear of having their taxes raised.*

Not only good architecture but outdoor sculpture and other art works visible to the public should be encouraged by public action. The Philadelphia Redevelopment Authority inserts a clause in all its contracts requiring the developer to provide appropriate fine arts in connection with all projects in amounts not less than one percent of the total dollar amount of the con-struction contract. This is a practice that should be made universal.

---

* The decision stood on appeal. See Joseph E. Seagram and Sons, Inc., vs. Tax Commission of the City of New York, 14 N.Y. 2nd 314, 251 N.Y.S. 2nd 460 (1965).

The public also has some right not to be affronted by ugly, vulgar, and overbearing outdoor signs. All outdoor signs should be limited by an enforced ordinance to a size and projection appropriate to the area and the building.

Boston is revising its obsolete building code, one of the greatest blocks to innovation in design. In many cities the revisions are whittled away by some of the building trades so that the new code and the old become indistinguishable. The supporters of the code revision here will have to persist in their efforts to prevent the same thing from happening in Boston.

Boston has not given the recognition that it should to the many courageous boards of trustees that have conferred benefits upon the public by employing great architects. In the metropolitan area there are examples of the work of Aalto, Belluschi, Gropius, Koch, Le Corbusier, Pei, Rudolph, Saarinen, Sert, Stubbins, and Yamasaki. This is a greater concentration of work by outstanding living architects than is to be found anywhere else in the world. We should have a Beauty Trail as well as a Freedom Trail to lead tourists and, above all, Bostonians to the works of these men as well as to the architectural and civic design achievements of an earlier day.

While adding to the beauties of Boston, we must take pains to preserve the heritage of the past. We should safeguard not only such well-known spots as Beacon Hill but also less well known ones, some of them of almost equal beauty, in Charlestown and in the North and South Ends.

So far we have discussed only visual beauty. There are other things that should be done to make Boston more attractive. One thing that should be done is to reduce noise and dirt. Few people are fully aware, we suspect, of the nerve-fraying and even demoralizing effects of such nuisances. For the most part, they work below the level of consciousness.

When it comes to dirt, in some of the poorer sections of Boston the streets and alleys are littered with refuse most of the time. There is no point in blaming this on the people who live in these districts. Most of them would like to have the streets and alleys clean. If the city will enforce the law against a few offenders and if it will provide reasonably good refuse collection and street cleaning service, as city officials say they intend to do, there will be a greater incentive for the individual citizen to

do his part also to improve the situation. The Citizens Committee for a Cleaner Boston, Inc., established with the encouragement of Mayor Collins, undoubtedly can help publicize a clean-up program.

The reduction of air pollution is another task to which the city should set itself more energetically.

More important in Boston, perhaps, would be the reduction of pollution in the river and bay so that the whole waterfront could be developed for recreation. To reduce pollution to such

23. Harvard across the Charles. Lois M. Bowen's camera has captured a scene where the river flows from north to south (left to right). The near bank is Boston, the far bank Cambridge. Left: two of the resident houses for Harvard College upperclassmen. Right: Peabody Terrace, the new apartments for married students (architect José Luis Sert).

a degree that it would be possible to swim in the water would be impractical for economic reasons, but it might not cost a great deal to make the water inoffensive to the nose in summer. If that were done, the present useless, run-down pier space

could be developed with facilities for small boats, picnic places, and wharf-side restaurants. So for that matter could the islands in the bay.

It would be foolish to maintain that any amount of civic beauty, however small, should take absolute priority over every other value (comfort and convenience, for example) however large. Sometimes it will be necessary to sacrifice beautiful buildings and beautiful—or even clean—streets in order to have other things that people value. Such exchanges must be made with great deliberation, however, and after careful efforts to measure all of the values that are involved. As the architectural quality of new building improves, the incentive to preserve the old will be less strong than it is now.

Finally, we should recognize that it is the form and shape of a city and especially the layout of its transportation network, and not particular buildings or even streets, that make the difference between a metropolitan sprawl and a beautiful city. As the Committee on Civic Design of the Boston Society of Archi-

24. M.I.T. across the Charles. Here the river has turned eastward and widened into a basin, and Miss Bowen's view is northward to Cambridge. The tall new structure, designed by I. M. Pei, houses the Massachusetts Institute of Technology's Center for Earth Sciences.

tects has recently pointed out, highways can create an awareness of city form. This is a lesson which Boston has helped to teach by the example of Route 128 and which it must not itself forget.

Boston, we predict, will be one of the most beautiful cities in the world a generation hence. It will not, however, be as beautiful as it might be. No city that is built by a free people will ever be a great work of art, for freedom allows the expression of bad taste as well as of good. Let us be reconciled to the prospect that we will make mistakes in civic design in the future as we have in the past. To the extent that a choice must be made between civic freedom and civic beauty, we trust that the former will be preferred. The great challenge for Boston is to pursue the two goals simultaneously.

Index

"Crisis view" of the city, 1–3
Culture, 58–59, 64, 65, 77, 109–110. *See also* Institutions

Democracy: and housing, 74; and lack of beauty in American cities, 105, 108, 117; and art, 109; mentioned, 1, 14, 26, 75. *See also* Freedom
Democrats, 13, 22
Detroit, 8, 55
Disneyland vehicles, 39, 40
Downtown Boston, 6, 32, 33, 35–36, 40, 51, 55, 60–67
Drug addiction, 59, 85–86, 89, 95

Eckstein, Otto, 9
"Economizing view" of the city, 7. *See also* Metropolitan areas
Economy, Boston, *see* Enterprise
Economy, national, *see* Income (rise of)
Education, *see* Schools; Teachers
Efficiency: of governmental functions, 15, 20, 25; of freight transportation, 43, 46, 51; of wholesaling, 64; of housing industry, 70, 73; of schools, 75. *See also* Technology
Employment: white-collar workers, 1, 63; bulk cargo, 44; textile plants, 54; of youth, 90–92; mentioned, 6. *See also* Enterprise
Enterprise, spirit of, in Boston: history, 53–57; the city's characteristics, 57–59; future, 59. *See also* Private enterprise; Trade; Industry
Executive Council, Governor's, 24
Exports, 44, 46
Expressways, *see* Highways
"Exurbanites," 36–37

Federal Bureau of Investigation (F.B.I.): crime statistics, 94, 96; mentioned, 100
Federal Bureau of Narcotics, 86
Federal Office Building, 111
Fee-for-service, *see* User charges
Fenway, the, 102
Finance Commission, 11, 79
Financial district, in aerial photo, 4
Firemen, 14, 91
Foley, William J., Jr., 92
Ford Foundation, 92
Freedom: of individual choice, 8, 39, 74, 117; of authors, 9; of government to act, 23, 29, 77, 78, 80. *See also* Civil liberty; Consumers; Democracy
Freight, *see* Transportation, freight

General Court (Massachusetts legislature), 11–12, 14, 29, 80; photo of Senate, 12
Government, federal, 27, 29, 70–73, 92
Government, local: and American political system, 1, 12; and city problems, 6; number of in Boston area, 18; advantages and disadvantages of, 20–21; cost of, 25–27; and tax collection, 30; and housing, 70. *See also* Home rule; Metropolitan areas
Government, metropolitan, 22–24

Government, state: interferes in local governments, 11–15; and American cities, 13; and agreements between local governments, 21; tax collection, 30; transportation, 35; metropolitan problems, 67; aid to schools, 80; mentioned, 58n. *See also* Massachusetts; Governor; General Court
Government Center, 61, 112; in aerial photo, 4; model of, 111
Governor: powers of city appointments, 11; jurisdiction over metropolitan area, 23–24; term of office, 24n
Graham, Donald, 9
Gropius, Walter, 113

Hannah, John, quoted, 91
Harvard University, photo, 114–115
Heliport, 42, 48
Hickey, Edward, 9
Highways, 21, 32, 42, 48, 116, 117. *See also* Automobiles; Central Artery; Traffic; Route 128
Home rule, 1, 12–13, 23; in Massachusetts, 11, 13–15
Horizon, quoted, 112
Housing, 68–74; substandard, 2, 68; downtown, 65–66; market, 69, 70, 73; federal insurance programs, 70–71; public, 71; codes, 71, 73; Housing and Urban Development Act of 1965, 73n; mentioned, 1, 27, 57. *See also* Slums; Building codes; Urban renewal
Hovercraft, 40, 41
Hughes, Helen, 9
Hyde Park, 85
Hydrofoil, 40, 41

Income: discretionary, 1; and market mechanism, 7; rise of, 38, 64, 65, 66, 77, 84, 93, 109; upper-income people, 38, 66, 77; spent on housing, 69; juvenile delinquency, 84–85; cultural level, 109; mentioned, 75. *See also* Low-income people; Middle-income people
Industrial parks, 48, 54–55
Industry: competition for among communities, 21, 30; in New England, 43–44; electronics, 49, 54–55, 56; textile, 53–54, 56; shoe, 53, 56; history of in Boston, 53–54; research-based, 54; military contracts, 55, 56; moves from downtown, 62; housing, 69–71, 73; automobile, 71; mentioned, 15
Inflation, 26, 80
Institutions, 30, 58, 60, 66. *See also* Culture
Investment, 27, 28, 47, 61, 68
Irish immigrants, 13

Jet Skimmer, photo of, 41
Juvenile delinquency, 84–86, 88–93. *See also* Crime

Kenmore Square, photo of, 33
Koch, Carl, 113

Index

121

This book is one of a series published under the auspices of the Joint Center for Urban Studies, a cooperative venture of the Massachusetts Institute of Technology and Harvard University. The Joint Center was founded in 1959 to do research on urban and regional problems. Participants have included scholars from the fields of architecture, business, engineering, city planning, economics, history, law, philosophy, political science, and sociology.

Publications of the Joint Center for Urban Studies

PUBLISHED BY HARVARD UNIVERSITY PRESS

The Intellectual versus the City: From Thomas Jefferson to Frank Lloyd Wright, by Morton and Lucia White, 1962

Streetcar Suburbs: The Process of Growth in Boston, 1870–1900, by Sam B. Warner, Jr., 1962

City Politics, by Edward C. Banfield and James Q. Wilson, 1963

Law and Land: Anglo-American Planning Practice, edited by Charles M. Haar, 1964

Location and Land Use: Toward a General Theory of Land Rent, by William Alonso, 1964

Poverty and Progress: Social Mobility in a Nineteenth Century City, by Stephan Thernstrom, 1964

Boston: The Job Ahead, by Martin Meyerson and Edward C. Banfield, 1966

The Myth and Reality of Our Urban Problems, by Raymond Vernon, 1966

PUBLISHED BY THE M.I.T. PRESS

The Image of the City, by Kevin Lynch, 1960

Housing and Economic Progress: A Study of the Housing Experiences of Boston's Middle-Income Families, by Lloyd Rodwin, 1961

Beyond the Melting Pot: The Negroes, Puerto Ricans, Jews, and Irish of New York City, by Nathan Glazer and Daniel Patrick Moynihan, 1963

The Historian and the City, edited by Oscar Handlin and John Burchard, 1963

The Federal Bulldozer, by Martin Anderson, 1964

The Future of Old Neighborhoods, by Bernard J. Frieden, 1964

Man's Struggle for Shelter in an Urbanizing World, by Charles Abrams, 1964

The View from the Road, by Donald Appleyard, Kevin Lynch, and John R. Myer, 1964

The Joint Center also publishes monographs and reports